PENGUIN

LEFT, RIGHT AND CENTRE

Nidhi Razdan is an eminent journalist and columnist.

LEFT, RIGHT AND CENTRE

The Idea of India

Edited by

Nidhi Razdan

PENGUIN BOOKS

An imprint of Penguin Random House

PENGUIN BOOKS

USA | Canada | UK | Ireland | Australia
New Zealand | India | South Africa | China

Penguin Books is part of the Penguin Random House group of companies
whose addresses can be found at global.penguinrandomhouse.com

Published by Penguin Random House India Pvt. Ltd
4th Floor, Capital Tower 1, MG Road,
Gurugram 122 002, Haryana, India

First published in Viking by Penguin Random House India 2017
Published in paperback in Penguin Books 2021

The views and opinions expressed in this book are the authors' own and the
facts are as reported by them which have been verified to the extent possible,
and the publishers are not in any way liable for the same.

ISBN 9780143455615

Typeset in Adobe Garamond Pro by Manipal Technologies Limited, Manipal
Printed at Replika Press Pvt. Ltd, India

www.penguin.co.in

For my parents, my strength and inspiration

Contents

Contents

Introduction

The New Normal: The Idea of India

NIDHI RAZDAN

We would start early. Normally, it would be the dead of winter in December. The day would begin with a bath with water heated on the kitchen stove. There were no electric geysers. There was pretty much no electricity either. Layers and layers of clothing were piled on to keep us warm. And then there was the drive through some of the most picturesque parts of Kashmir, with my brother and I fighting for the front seat of the jeep. This is one of my earliest childhood memories—going back to Kashmir in the 1980s. Almost every year, in December, my parents, my younger brother and I would travel to Tul Mul or the revered Kheer Bhawani temple in Ganderbal, just outside Srinagar. This is one of the most sacred temples for Kashmiri Pandits. Here, the goddess Ragnya Devi or Maharagya Devi is on top of a pillar in the middle of a small pond. The spring water in the pond is known to change colour from time to time, and legend has it that the colour turns dark when something bad is about to happen. The story goes that many Pandits saw the water turn black just before militancy broke out, leading to the exodus of Pandits in 1989–90. An ominous foreboding of what lay ahead. At the shrine, we would follow my mother during her parikrama, and then do a traditional *aarti*. Before leaving, we would eat delicious *lucchis* made by local Muslim cooks. This was a ritual and probably the main reason why I loved going to Tul Mul and still do.

On the way back, there was another ritual. We would stop at the famous Hazratbal Shrine in Srinagar. My father made it a point to do this on each and every visit. We would go inside and say our prayers. My parents always told us that this was what true Kashmiriyat was about. About Hindus and Muslims respecting each other's religions. These visits took place at a time when we lived abroad and would come visiting India every year. Worried that their almost teenaged children would turn into American brats, my parents believed it was important to teach us that this is what Kashmir stood for, and, on a bigger scale, that this is what India stood for. This was my idea of India as I was growing up.

Then one day in 1989, as militancy was just beginning in the Kashmir Valley, my father made his way to Hazratbal. But this time it was different. There was a sign in the lane leading to the shrine which said that non-Muslims would not be allowed in. My anguished father stared at that sign for several minutes, completely taken aback. Someone walked up to him and said, 'You must be a non-Muslim.'

'Yes,' my father replied. 'What has happened to Kashmir?' he asked.

The man turned around and said, 'Come with me, let me see who will stop you.' And they went inside.

The sign was a reflection of what was happening in Kashmir at the time, with the hounding of the Kashmiri Pandit community.

It was on this day, for the very first time, I realized that my idea of a perfect India was flawed. It was confusing, complex and not peppered with the idealism that I had grown up with.

My close family fled Kashmir in January 1990, when the mass exodus of the Pandit community took place. My grandparents, my uncle and cousins literally packed their bags overnight and ran away, fearing for their lives. Many years later, in the year 2000, I returned to Kashmir as a young reporter with NDTV. My parents were terrified. They had not gone back in over ten years. My mother told me never to wear a bindi, never to say my last name as that would give away my identity and never to speak in Kashmiri, a language I had grown up loving. The worst of the militancy was over but the curfews and restrictions were still daily phenomena.

When I reached Srinagar, many people already recognized me from television. They knew I was a Kashmiri Pandit. At first I was wary, my mother's fears ringing in my head. But very soon that fear dissipated. I was welcomed warmly, like a long-lost daughter who had finally come home. And with that, my faith in the idea of Kashmiriyat and the idea of India was restored, just a little. Over the next many many years as I travelled regularly to report on Kashmir, I never felt scared. Local residents only gave me their love and blessings. Some went out of their way to help me.

When India celebrated its sixtieth Independence day in 2007, I went to film a documentary on what young people in Kashmir wanted, what their aspirations were. This was a generation that had grown up in more than twenty years of militancy. But all of them had aspirations like any other eighteen- or twenty-year-old in India. They wanted to do MBAs at good universities, live in Delhi or Mumbai. President Kalam was an idol, John Abraham, the film hero, was admired. But this was also a generation that grew up with guns and bombs, encounters and curfews. They also grew up without Kashmiri Pandits. It was heartbreaking to go to the old neighbourhoods where Pandits once lived, to meet people whose teenaged children had no idea who or what a Kashmiri Pandit was. A university student stunned me during an interview when she said that she did not even consider Pandits as 'real Kashmiris'. It made me angry and I argued with her, calling her out for her ignorance.

On the other side, young Pandits have grown up in exile, bitter and angry about the way they, their parents and grandparents were driven out of the Valley, and the way their relatives and loved ones were killed and targeted. Their anger is deep and real. The wounds have not healed and still run deep.

Today, the discourse about Kashmir has become part of the neo-nationalism of our times. We say Kashmir belongs to India and yet it is almost as if the rest of India has abandoned the Kashmiri people. There is no attempt to understand their alienation and pain. There is no political outreach. The UPA government paid lip service to an interlocutor's report prepared after the 2010 unrest. It wasn't even discussed in the Parliament. A mistake acknowledged by former Home Minister P. Chidambaram. Today's 'nationalist' narrative has only increased the distance between New Delhi and Kashmir. Many Kashmiri Pandits, who have now spent over twenty-five years in exile, want to return home but only if they will be safe. They are not a big vote bank, so no government has really seriously listened to their concerns or acted on them.

The tragedy of Kashmir is that the violence has affected all the communities. From Pandits to Muslims. Most hardliners on either side sneer at any equivalence. Nevertheless, the fact is that weighing one community's pain over another's has helped no one.

During 2016's summer unrest, 12,000 people were injured, as per official figures. Seven thousand of these were pellet gun injuries. Many of them children. The forces have an extremely tough job in the Kashmir Valley, as they deal with Pakistan-backed terror and often hostile crowds who throw stones with a view to kill. But blinding innocents is not how the rest of India will win the hearts of Kashmiris. In the last year alone, official figures show, eighty-eight local boys have joined militant units. In 2015, that number was sixty-six and just sixteen in 2013. Many of them, like Hizbul Mujahideen's Burhan Wani, were educated bright young men, who were doing well in school.

Today, India's biggest threat in Jammu and Kashmir comes from within, and Pakistan is taking advantage of that. But there is little or no acknowledgement of the dangers of this homegrown terror. Of course, Pakistan has a big role to play in fomenting trouble, but we need to ask ourselves why ordinary Kashmiris are coming out in large numbers to attend the funerals of terrorists. Kashmir is a very complex story. Nuance is lost on many of those who parachute in to cover the state as journalists, trying to understand it in very narrow and simplistic terms. The same large crowds have come out for the funerals of local policemen and army men.

In 2007, when I was filming my documentary in Srinagar, there were massive protests. But they were not for 'azaadi' or freedom. They were for jobs. The UPA government just didn't seize the moment. This was a great opportunity for the Centre to take some real political initiatives in Kashmir. They didn't. But jobs are only part of the problem. There is a deep political issue that needs engagement, but in these nationalist times, it is not fashionable or politically correct to talk about alienation. Tourism is measured as an index of normality. Over 65 per cent of Kashmiris braced boycotts and threats to vote in the last assembly election in 2014. It was the highest voter turnout in twenty-five years, according to the Election Commission. They did the same in 2008, with a turnout of 61.42 per cent. This doesn't mean Kashmiris have necessarily found common ground with New Delhi. But it means they are willing to have a say in their future and who governs them. We need to build on that, on their trust in the political process.

The chest-thumping narrative on Kashmir is part of the larger nationalist narrative we are increasingly seeing in India. Today, you have to wear your patriotism on your sleeve. You have to wear it on social media, in television debates, even in the cinema. To question the government, the courts, the army is to be anti-national. To differ, is to be unpatriotic. It's my patriotism versus yours.

This is a narrative that even India's courts, including the mighty Supreme Court, have fed into. How else can one explain the judgment on standing up for the national anthem in movie halls? In a country where there are reports of over 30 million cases pending before the courts, it is rather incredible that the

Supreme Court had time to pronounce judgments on what constitutes their brand of nationalism. Or, for that matter, to hear public interest litigations on 'sardarji jokes'.

And so the country's top court said in 2016 that all cinemas have to play the national anthem before a film is screened 'for the love of the motherland'. Those in the hall must stand up and all doors must be closed so that people don't move around.

'These days, people read things that have nothing to do with nationalism but don't study material related to nationalism,' said a bench headed by justice Dipak Misra.

'Universalism is all right but still Bharat is the epitome of culture, knowledge . . . *gyaan* and *vigyaan* . . . people should feel that they live in a nation and show respect to the national anthem and the national flag,' said the learned court.

Imagine the fear of being lynched in a movie hall if you don't stand up for the anthem. It happened to a disabled man in Goa, who couldn't believe it when the punches came raining down. Award-winning writer Salil Chaturvedi, who suffers from spinal injury, could not get up, and he was thrashed by a couple standing in the aisle above him.

This is 'the new normal'.

Where nationalism has been reduced to forcing people to sing the national anthem. It is about outraging when the national flag is on a T-shirt. Americans burn their national flag all the time. But they won't be arrested for it.

Ironically, the man who wrote India's national anthem, Rabindranath Tagore, was the one who called nationalism a 'great menace'. In fact, throughout his life, Tagore was deeply critical of nationalism as a concept. Mahatma Gandhi famously did not agree with him. But if he were alive today, Tagore would have probably been branded an anti-national too. He said of nationalism:

> India has never had a real sense of nationalism. Even though from childhood I had been taught that the idolatry of nation is almost better than reverence for god and humanity, I believe I have outgrown that teaching, and it is my conviction that my countrymen will gain truly their India by fighting against that education which teaches them that a country is greater than the ideals of humanity.

What is incredible is that Tagore, nearly 100 years ago, saw the pitfalls of nationalism, and we are struggling to understand it even today. He had also said: 'Nationalism is the training of a whole people for a narrow ideal; and when it gets hold of their minds, it is sure to lead them to moral degeneracy and intellectual blindness.'

'The new normal' is one in which the media, along with the judiciary, has joined the nationalist bandwagon. Where spin is news, where opinion becomes fact. Where TV anchors and reporters stand in flak jackets in their newsrooms and cry for war with Pakistan or with those deemed to be 'undermining the nation'. Through their chest-thumping nationalism, they shout for blood to be shed and shout down those who ask for peace and dialogue. Where Kashmiri guests who speak of alienation are verbally thrashed and called separatists. Where hashtags like #WeStandWithSoldiers or #PakistanCornered have reduced television news to a mockery. Where those who say 'soldiers died in an encounter' are abused on social media for not using the word 'martyr'.

Look at the media's reporting of the 2016 surgical strikes. There was very little questioning of the official narrative. I am not saying the strikes did not happen. But did we, as journalists, ask all the right questions? Instead, some of us stood in mini 'war rooms' created on TV sets, showing viewers how the strikes 'really happened', and then proceeded to call for Pakistan's annihilation. Several different figures were leaked to the press about the number of casualties on the other side. But all off the record. Why didn't the media demand more accountability on sensitive stories like these? Much of what was broadcast or printed in the days following the strikes was 'off the record'. We should have insisted on greater transparency and on record statements. To even ask these questions now raises the 'anti-national', 'unpatriotic' war cry. Because, after all, we must never question that citadel known as the armed forces. Except that we MUST. In a democracy, we must question all institutions and hold them accountable. Whether that is the army or the courts.

India suffered a series of terror strikes in 2016 on its security installations, from the attack on the Pathankot airbase to the army units in Uri and Nagrota, all of which saw major casualties. According to the government, in a written response to a question in the Lok Sabha, Subhash Bhamre, minister of state for defence, said ten cases of attacks on the army were recorded in 2014, followed by eleven in 2015, fifteen in 2016 and three until 15 March this year. Sixty-eight army soldiers were killed in 2016, up from thirty-eight in 2014.

A report of a tri-services panel, headed by former army Vice Chief Lt Gen. Philip Campose, had raised an alarm about the existing security infrastructure post Pathankot. The panel had submitted its report to the then defence minister in May 2016, saying, 'The security set-up is quite poor in most places, with command and control problems and ambiguous SOPs, without specific responsibilities and responses being assigned to personnel. The guards at the bases are poorly equipped. Sentries continue to use outdated INSAS rifles, which are no match for the AK-47s of terrorists. Most sentries and quick-reaction teams do not have bullet-proof jackets or "patkas" and night-vision devices.'

But India's lack of preparedness to deal with suicide attacks is hardly debated in our news media, barring a few. To me, that is the single most anti-national act we can do, by not asking tough questions on why our military installations are not safer and why they keep coming under attack.

This is 'the new normal'. As comedian Tanmay Bhat aptly put it in one of his videos post demonetization, 'Soldier bol diya na, soldier. Ab bas.' Once you invoke the soldier, there is nothing anyone can say. It has spawned some jokes, such as, 'how can you worry about your Aadhaar card, when soldiers are fighting along the Line of Control' or 'how can you worry about your flight being late when soldiers are fighting at the border?'

It is now anti-national to even question the government. So most TV channels today simply don't do it. In an interview to NDTV, Arun Shourie called them 'North Korean TV channels' that essentially parrot the government line. The raids on the NDTV in June marked a turning point for free press in India.

As Shourie said, it was meant to 'kill the chicken to frighten the monkeys', quoting a Chinese proverb.[1] When the ruling party cites Indira Gandhi's Emergency, I want to remind them that that is exactly what we never want repeated, declared or undeclared. Today, anyone who questions the establishment, the army, the courts, is branded a traitor, a Naxal, or, god forbid, a Lutyens' liberal.

Strident nationalism and chants of 'Bharat mata ki jai' are now 'the new normal'. Worship of the cow is 'the new normal'. 'The new normal' is the new world of post truth or 'alternative facts'. To justify drowning out voices of dissent and disagreement by those who can shout louder. 'The new normal' is where the country's largest state is headed by a man whose claim to fame is a hard-line Hindutva rhetoric, calling for 'take 100 Muslim girls for one Hindu girl they take'.

As we debate these issues on television night after night, I have often asked whether, after seventy years of independence, India is an insecure nation. Do we feel easily threatened by dissent, by slogans because we are inherently insecure? India has weathered many storms and insurgencies in the past seventy years. But with all our problems and warts, we have largely remained a united, thriving, vibrant nation. But I wonder whether we are deeply insecure in our core.

Our universities have been great spaces for debate and dissent for decades. But 'the new normal' does not allow it. The unrest on our campuses has grown. Seminars are the new anti-nationals;

---

[1] NDTV, 6 June 2017, www.ndtv.com/video/shows/reality-check/truth-coheres-falsehood-falls-apart-arun-shourie-to-ndtv-459370.

especially if they have been organized on Kashmir. With its students, Kanhaiya Kumar and Umar Khalid accused of sedition (though yet to be chargesheeted), Jawaharlal Nehru University (JNU) has become the new anti-national monolith, in one giant stroke.

Social media warriors are the most strident in expressing their patriotism; especially those who live in Seattle and New Jersey, giving free advice on how the motherland must live, giving all of us lessons on nationalism.

A feisty, young, intelligent woman was trolled on social media earlier this year for having a point of view on India-Pakistan ties.

It began when she took a stand on the bullying on campus by the ABVP, the student wing of the RSS. She was attacked online not just for her stand on the ABVP, but also for a video she had posted online last year where she talked about the death of her father, a soldier, in Kashmir at the hands of Pakistani terrorists. But she wanted peace with Pakistan, not war. Big mistake.

Gurmehar Kaur was hounded on social media. Even worse, she was mocked by a senior minister. When Minister of State for Home Affairs Kiren Rijiju asked on Twitter 'who is polluting Gurmehar Kaur's mind', he assumed she was too dumb to have a mind of her own, attributing political motives.

She had made a video last year about the death of her father, a soldier, who died in an encounter shortly after the Kargil war in 1999. In that video, Gurmehar was trying to make a bigger point about peace. Those attacking her called her out for one line: 'Pakistan did not kill my dad, war killed him.' But in the full video she says, 'I was two years old when my father died . . . I remember how much I hated Pakistanis because they killed my father . . . When I was six years old, I tried to stab a lady in a burka because for some strange reason, I thought she was responsible for my father's death . . . my mother held me back and made me understand that Pakistan did not kill my dad, war killed him.'

Gurmehar's mother 'polluted' her mind. She was trying to teach her daughter not to hate the people of Pakistan for what happened to her father.

In the age of Twitter, it takes only minutes for fiction to become fact, for people to be bullied and mocked for having a point of view, for abuse and threats to take a life of their own.

It brings me back to the words of Rabindranath Tagore. He had passionately written in 1937 against any attempt to curb free speech and thought. He wrote, 'It would be an uninteresting but a sterile world of mechanical regularity if all our opinions were forcibly made alike . . . Opinions are constantly changed and re-changed only through free circulation of intellectual forces and persuasion. Violence begets violence and blind stupidity. Freedom of mind is needed for the reception of truth; terror hopelessly kills it.'

As India turns seventy, I am hopeful that somewhere Tagore's words will ring true for most of us. As the country continues to grapple with multiple discourses, in this book thinkers from the Left, a considerable sum from the Right and an impressive lot from the Centre offer politically charged, argumentative and diverse views of their 'idea of India'.

In his 1916 novel, *The Home and the World*, Tagore wrote, 'I am willing to serve my country; but my worship I reserve for Right which is far greater than country. To worship my country as a god is to bring a curse upon it.'

On the Wrong Side of History

SHAH FAESAL

Shah Faesal is a medical doctor-turned-civil servant from Srinagar. He writes on issues related to economic development, conflict resolution, and Kashmiri culture and heritage.

With great fear comes the great urge to rush to the washroom. As a child I had seen my parents quibble over the need to avoid going out late at night to answer nature's call, more so when the dogs barked. Relentless barking of the canines always meant movement of gunmen through the thickets in our backyard. Suddenly in the middle of dinner, the rustling of withered maize stems, whistle of a wayward cicada or a thud of fence-jumping cats would alert and freeze all of us; if Father had picked up a morsel of food from the plate, he would wait with an open mouth and a slight tremor running down his elbow and gesture towards me to stop sounding the crockery and be attentive. We used to be told stories of days, long gone, when a person could walk alone through the village even after midnight. Things had changed. Till a few years back, dogs barked non-stop like that only when fiery-eyed panthers prowled about in the nearby apple orchards on Thursday nights; panthers, mistakenly called *seh* (lions), would come down from the woods to engage in zikr near the holy mound.

We believed dogs to be prescient creatures who howled at the time of azan because they could see Satan escape the call of the faithful coming out from the mosque's pulpit; they went berserk right before earthquakes struck because they perceived what men could not; and dogs, those ordinary self-trained street dogs, recognized the sulphur odour of Kalashnikovs from long distances and filled scary nights with deafening noise. But the irony was that in spite of being everywhere, each hamlet having its own contingent of large-sized bear-like dogs, these animals were strictly forbidden to enter our homes and perhaps no one in our village owned a dog.

We believed that if a family owned a pet, then angels, who were supposed to home-deliver divine mercy, would avoid visiting that household. In fact, when one day we had to replace the old ceiling fan in our drawing room, a pious family friend objected and said that its blades had an embossed dog-like marking so it should be avoided. We changed the fan and got another one with a paisley mark. Our spiritual economics could not ignore what descended from the sky. So it was a strange love-hate relationship with animals. They were friends, much like the other parties of war—soldiers and militants—but only as long as they remained at a safe distance from the threshold.

In keeping with the traditional architecture, those days, we had a dry toilet constructed at a distance from the house where instead of toilet paper or water, small lumps of good earth were used for cleaning; at the end of the year the night soil was dug out and spread in the undulating cornfields. It was a taboo to build toilets inside the house as it created some sort of a *vastu* problem. We believed that a toilet close to the kitchen affected

Barakah—the heavenly bliss that manifested as abundance of food and absence of famine. But this changed soon afterwards.

Our understanding of Islam included many myths that found no mention in the Holy Quran and were purely cultural beliefs that kept adding to the great river of Islam as it flowed from Arabia to Kashmir. Similar was the case with keeping dogs at bay, although Islamic tradition notes the example of Qitmeer, the legendary dog who was the trusted companion of the People of the Cave, the Islamic version of the Seven Sleepers of Ephesus.

We would have our ears to the ground all the time and every howl, every hiss had a meaning. Those were the initial days of militancy and fear of gunmen loomed large. Distant footfalls of soldiers on night patrol would immediately make our hearts pound and even a friendly knock at the door or a hallucinatory cry in the dark would loosen our bowels. We never knew when and where the two sides might confront each other, leading to killings and a crackdown the morning after. Fear ruled minds and it ruled the bowels too. Later, it was this fear that compelled us to re-engineer our timber houses and fit sanitary commodes in bathrooms, although old people, reluctant to accept the change, would still block the flush pipes with clay.

I had grown up with both fire and fear in my belly. I wanted to do something big in life, and I was ready to work hard for that. So at that precise moment when my UPSC results were to be declared, I was, as expected, exerting myself in the toilet in my Delhi apartment, playing with the water tap, scrolling up and down the result window on my Nokia phone, waiting for the result link to go green. It was a moment of reckoning for me, not because this was the biggest test of my life but because at that moment, I felt I had closed all my doors and there was no going back. When I had decided that I would quit medicine and pursue a career in administration, my friends had mocked me. First, it was a very unfashionable switch, medicine was a noble profession, and then everyone believed that being a Kashmiri youngster my dream of joining the bureaucracy of India would soon come crashing down as Indian institutions were by default prejudiced against Kashmiri Muslims. But for me it was not about choosing the right career. It was a part of the larger search to find meaning in the chaos around.

I came from a family of fence sitters. Right from the onset of militancy we had tried to be equidistant from the militants and soldiers, when in an atmosphere of war it was a rather awkward thing to do. People boldly took sides for the sake of survival. For ordinary people there was no free will at all. Some of our neighbours became militant sympathizers and bought rations for them. Some became friends with the army, mainly because it gave them access to cheap goods in the CSD canteens. The more intelligent ones enjoyed both worlds. But very few people stayed aloof and the non-partisan citizens wrongly believed that innocent bystanders would not be hurt in the 'just' war. Jihad had a divine sanction, we believed in those days, and we were quite confident that god was on our side.

What we had forgotten was that turmoil, a euphemism for a bloody war, would not distinguish good men from bad men, armed from unarmed, cowards from courageous and combatants from bystanders. We wrongly expected soldiers to spare our elderly men and women when they were on a beating spree in the hamlet. We hoped that militants would first judiciously inquire, before hanging civilians alleged to have gone against the cause. I had seen at close quarters the ruthlessness with which power was exercised by those who had suddenly got hold of our lives, and I wanted to change that system. It was a quixotic aspiration but, nevertheless, it was there.

That night when 'unidentified gunmen' came to kill my father, he was watching the evening news on an old black-and-white television kept in our newly refurbished kitchen. Dinner was about to be served when two tall non-Kashmiri-looking young men knocked at the door. Terrified, my mother gathered her nerves and unlatched the door; two men, smiling, appeared in the doorway at once. They walked in with their boots on, as combatants were not expected to remove their shoes, asked for a glass of water and kept standing; my father also stood there out of courtesy. Even though they frequented our neighbourhood, gunmen rarely came to our house. We were a happy household because we were indifferent to war. But we were known to be a meek household where children cried on seeing gunmen, so we had not been extended the privilege of friendship by both soldiers and militants. We never complained.

As was the pattern with all civilian killings by unidentified gunmen, my father was asked to walk to the next room so that something confidential could be discussed. My mother knew that the other room always meant the other world; she guessed it well and politely said that whatever had to be discussed should be done in her presence, right there. The gunmen smiled and sipped water and then politely gave up the idea of a conversation and sought permission to leave. It was a gesture of courtesy to seek ceremonial permission to leave and this cheered up my mother. She thought that they were actually friendly gunmen and this even tempted her to talk about her brother who was a celebrated commander. But she was wary because she wasn't sure if this name-dropping would help or if it was a safe thing to do with these armed strangers. So, my father walked ahead to see them off as part of the tradition to accompany guests for at least three steps towards the exit. It was also a reciprocation of the courtesy they had earlier displayed. But as the door was about to shut, the gunmen poked the barrel through the cleft; there was a click and two bullets hit his chest and one hit the television. Within seconds, my father was dead. He had been killed with all possible courtesy.

Next morning, our village saw the first-ever protest against the 'unidentified gunmen'. My father was a renowned teacher of that area and was known as someone who was politically non-partisan, soft-mannered and one who 'sweated in the presence of his elders'. This sweating was a cultural symbol of noble behaviour, and I had often seen pearls of perspiration on my father's forehead when he came across people whom he respected or was in awe of. He was a brilliant, self-made man, a polymath who spoke many languages. He had dropped out of engineering college because he could not afford the third semester fee. But he was shy and would often tell me that he wanted me to grow up without the cold sweat on my face. His killing had forced locals to do the unthinkable—to seek answers from those who ruled the streets at that time. His funeral procession was attended by people from all over the district; during those years of conflict the only symbol of a man's success was the size of his funeral crowd.

Later that day, a group of elders came down from the woods and apologized to my mother in the presence of the entire village for the 'mischief' done by a few lower cadres without informing the high command. Civilian killings were not unusual and anyone seen to be supportive of the Indian establishment or anyone who even appeared to be indifferent to the Kashmir cause would figure on the hit list, much like anyone seen as a militant sympathizer or a Jamaat ideologue would be shot by state forces without much regret.

Such was the helplessness that we were not even sure who had killed him, true to the prediction made by the Prophet of Islam (PBUH) that there will be a time when an innocent person won't know why he was killed and the killer won't know why he killed him. So this apology had done us a great favour. It could not resurrect my father's dead body, but it saved us from the possible taint that my father was killed for going against the Kashmir movement. Killing was not a problem in Kashmir. The stigma was. It was not an honourable thing to die as an Indian in Kashmir. It ruled out a place in paradise for the dead person, where only those who stood for the 'cause' could go. A fortnight later, the severed head of a local young man was found perched on one of the iron grills around martyrs' graveyard in the main town. We received an unsigned note that said that my innocent father's murder had been avenged by slaying the man who had masterminded the murder; he had violated the organizational policy for bystanders. It was a justice rarely done. We got a closure. We were lucky unlike thousands of others who disappeared mysteriously or got killed by this side or that, but never understood why and how it had happened.

The parting kiss on my father's cold forehead broke something inside me permanently. I couldn't believe that a person like him could also get killed. He had religiously followed the survival manual for bystanders. He was anonymous, he had no opinion on anything overtly political, and he was a very ordinary, unambitious family man. But for the first time in my life I realized that in a war there were no bystanders. There was no neutrality. I felt the pain of all those fellow sufferers who had lost their dear ones either to bullets of the state or to bullets of the non-state. That day I lost appetite for political rhetoric and poetry that glorified war and its perpetrators. As people started counting us with the other orphans in the village and began making predictions about how our household would come crumbling down with the loss of its anchor, I realized that at the end of the day it really didn't matter who killed whom, but what mattered was that Kashmiris were dying for just being out there while the two countries were sorting out some unfinished business of history between them.

I had always seen militancy as an aberration. Although, by the time I finished high school, it had been there for more than a decade, but all of us still knew that it was at the most a short-lived emotional meltdown. It was not going to be a permanent feature of our social and political lives. New or old militancy, it was wrong to say that Kashmiris were dying because they wanted to. No one likes dying. Kashmiris were always non-militant, peace-loving people by nature, so much so that colonial historians made the mistake of interpreting our collective forbearance as cowardice. A decade was not a long time but we had already begun to miss the pre-1989 days of calm, cultural life of the Kashmiri Pandits, harvest songs, nightly recitals of *Gulrez*, evening shows at the local cinema and street performances by turbaned trumpeters.

The peak was past us. We had seen giantlike, fearless militant commanders coming and quietly fading away. Crackdowns and encounters were becoming less frequent. The war theatre was done with characters such as Mast Gul who set ablaze the most venerated shrine of Kashmir at Chrar and then walked with guns blazing through the city back to his home. Jawala Singh, a major, who used to single-handedly thrash a crowd of hundreds coming from Friday prayers in our village, was also a thing of the past. We had been witness to large machine guns being collected along with driftwood when a flash flood came down from nearby hills, unexploded hand grenades gathered among pine cones by unsuspecting woodcutters; the storm that had sucked in thousands of Kashmiri youth was losing wind and gradually taking a new shape.

Gun was inherently an unsustainable option, and militancy came with an expiry date. It didn't have structures to perpetuate the violence from one generation to another. Ironically, that privilege belonged to the state. A soldier's gun butt and a cop's baton were memory aids of a history that seemed unchanging and had violence as its core. I was too young to understand the grievances that people had against the state. But I had seen men from my village rising against the 'system' by going towards the woods and donning the rebel fatigues. I was a pacifist and wanted to be a part of the 'system'. My friends wanted to wreck the system from outside, and I wanted to humanize it from within. It was idealism on both sides, and each one of us was a fool as we would realize a little later.

Nevertheless, my selection into the civil service surprised many, including me, although I had a feeling that something big was coming my way. I had really worked hard throughout my life. But for this exam, I had pushed myself to the edge. I had prepared while battling the hellish heat of Delhi summer; there can be nothing worse for a Kashmiri who is used to cold weather. It's like sending a penguin to an equatorial school for flight training. I stayed in a small room; shuffling piles of books around me, reading what was unreadable and understanding what I found had little significance either to my future or the future of the country. But since the exam demanded knowing a little bit about almost everything under the sky, I didn't know what to skip and what to keep. I took it as an opportunity to read and read and read whatever came my way. It was a middle-class dream that would instantly catapult me into a rarefied stratum of the society where there was power and from where lives were controlled. But more than that it was an urge to access the leak in the sky from where miseries of common people, more so the fence sitters, came trickling down. I wanted to see for myself what had degenerated the state into a man-eating monster that had no goodwill for its subjects. I knew what was wrong with the militants, but I wanted to know what was wrong with the state.

It was a strange coincidence that my result came at a time when the Valley was witnessing yet another civilian agitation. People were dying, and stone pelting at all the symbols of the state authority that had been a common refrain during all preceding agitations was happening with renewed vigour. In fact, other than the brief pauses we called normality, we had been witnessing long periods of turbulence throughout, and summers had become the most opportune time to fight it out. The 1931 agitation had also happened in the month of July, but since the onset of militancy, each and every day of spring and summer saw commemorations of killings of well-known and lesser-known sons of the soil. The calendar of memories had countless red-letter days, red colour in our part of the world being indicative of sacrifice. The loss on all sides had been so great that every occasion was an occasion for mourning, and a land that had lost its sons and lovers appeared to be in a state of perpetual bereavement.

Yet there was a meaning to how things happened in Kashmir and the timing of it all. I became a hero overnight, and the story of a schoolteacher's son from a lesser-known village who went on to become the first Kashmiri topper of the Indian civil service generated a lot of interest in Kashmir. First, it was a classic rags-to-riches story. Relatives who had long forgotten us came around, new friendships with the local elite were formed, invitation cards to wedding ceremonies of unknown people started arriving by post and middlemen with matrimonial proposals from renowned families of the city gathered outside my rented accommodation in Srinagar. Deep inside I laughed all the time, pinching myself, noticing every new gesture from the people around, the new flare of emotion on their faces, the stiff body language of the visitors who suddenly found themselves inferior to me in official status although I was yet to be assigned an office. For the occasion I took to suits and ties because everyone wanted this boy to look like a gentleman.

Second, it was the Kashmiri pride that made an otherwise ordinary thing look really big. I had topped at the country level and it was symbolic of a Kashmiri showing the rest of the world that we were not behind anyone else. Expectedly, the media found a great story in my success and going with the mood of the times, rather than talking about my personal struggle, interviewed me about the turmoil, youth aspirations, India-Pakistan relationship, peace and conflict as if I had not been appointed to a government office but to a political assignment. My success was instantly connected with the politics of the place. I became famous because I was a Kashmiri. Although I tried my best to stay away from controversial topics and unnecessary limelight, time and again my name would be dragged in because the discourse was such that my selection was portrayed as a resolution. It was unintended and spontaneous. I was the new role model to be shown to fellow Kashmiris. A purely individual achievement became a hotspot on the timeline of war.

It continued to be so till almost a month later when I met an old man at a university felicitation who came running towards me after I had finished my address to the students—who aspired to seek positions in the government—in the packed auditorium. Without any hesitation he told me that he couldn't believe that I had cleared that exam on my own but now that he had heard my speech it had somehow convinced him that I was not a state-sponsored *sadhbhavana* topper. I was shocked but I smiled back while he took my autograph on his phone diary for his children at home. He was well meaning and had given me a compliment, howsoever strange it had sounded. For his honesty I hugged him. But this was an introduction to an altogether unknown realm of public perception around my selection that I had missed in the midst of celebrations. While I was being carried on shoulders with cardamom garlands around my neck, in the other corner of the street I was being discussed for very different reasons.

There were many questions. How could a Kashmiri Muslim top an all-India level exam when not many had done this before? How could the son of an ordinary schoolteacher do it? How could a boy from an average family do it? Did it have anything to do with the death of his father a long time back? Was it just clever perception management? Was it related to the ongoing agitation and an effort to distract the youth from stone pelting? Did he really have the ability to qualify for this exam? Was it part of a new policy of the Government of India to bring Kashmiris into the mainstream? One by one, these questions unfolded in front of me.

It saddened me initially. I felt as if my struggle was not being respected, as if this dismissal was part of some small-town jealousy, as if these whispers had something to do with my modest pedigree. Otherwise why would the Valley's elite have questions about a random thing like the selection of a youngster from a rural setting in a fiercely competitive examination. I would look at my batchmates from other states and envy them for not having to face all that we had to face in Kashmir. It was hard to explain to my non-Kashmiri friends what it meant to be rejected back home while the rest of the country celebrated you.

It hurt me and gave way to self-doubt and negative energy that had the potential to bring me down. During my professional training, I became gloomy and there were times when I thought of giving up and doing something even bigger that might convince people that I had achieved this on my own. But then I realized that I couldn't keep listening to people who didn't matter to me at all. I pulled myself together, remembered the days of my struggle, talked to myself in silence, got support from my family and gathered the courage to take criticism with a smile. There was so much unfair criticism—what we now call 'criticism-*fisabilillah*'—that I eventually stopped fearing it, and instead recalled my father's words that whatever the situation I must learn to reciprocate evil with goodness, criticism with compassion. It was not easy but I learnt to smile in spite of the odds and it made my life easy. I took things in my stride and focused on my work as a civil servant, trying to bring cheer to forlorn faces, working for the victims of turmoil, engaging with schoolchildren and absorbing the goodness around me.

Kashmiri minds have always been susceptible to doubts. Centuries of contestation with the state and a culture of political uncertainty have eliminated trust from the society; colonial historians reinforced an inferiority complex by calling Kashmiris *badzaat*, crooked, bad-mouthed, selfish wretches; and the violent conflict destroyed whatever else was left of us. We were made to accept that we were a good-for-nothing people. In all the things happening around us, rather than forces of nature or forces of economics, it was the state that moved its chessmen around us from behind the curtains. Elite gossip was that one needed political expediency and not merit to win elections, get leaders dismissed, for college admissions, appointments into government services, allotment of petty contracts, and for conferring of bravery awards. All success stories were sponsored; culture was a distraction; education was a conspiracy; all sports were anti-resistance; all stories in the media were planted. Kashmir sought refuge in a self-imposed dystopia that helped explain many things which could not be explained otherwise. But in an environment of suspicion, these perceptions and questions were quite normal. People could not be blamed for heeding conspiracy theories. The state did have in its closet rotting facsimiles related to military operations gone wrong, ridiculously thoughtless political manoeuvrings, weird attempts at social engineering, and rejected manuals of perception management. It was not fair to blame public memory. The state had made many mistakes in the past.

When there was a grenade blast in my village, people would debate whether the person who had been seen throwing the hand grenade was really the accused or his lookalike; whether he worked for the agency he claimed he worked for or he was a double agent. Then there were 'unidentified gunmen', shady anonymous assassins who would kill at will without the fear of being brought to account. People didn't even know what to condemn and what not to condemn, what to blame on the state and what to blame on the non-state. Nothing was certain. Recently a spymaster said in his book that nothing is straight in Kashmir except the poplars.

An environment of fear brings along a culture of alienation and paranoia. At one level it has broken relationships between the state and the people. But at the core of it there is loss of trust and faith between the people themselves. I remember the general impression that people had in our village was that everyone was an agent on somebody's payroll. People talked in whispers lest a third person overheard it and complained to those in charge. It went to the next level where people stopped talking to one another at all, scared that the other person might be an army agent or militants' agent or agent of so many other 'agencies' that worked in the background.

Kashmir had seen the Stalinist culture of *Kontreh-Pandah* (29.15) or *Khoftan-Faqeer* in the 1950s, the rogue secret police that were paid Rs 29.15 per month, hence the name. But after the onset of militancy, we developed an 'agent consciousness' that was part of the larger process of disempowerment that we had seen as a people. From being the 'principal' to becoming 'agents' of one party or the other, Kashmiris were made to believe that they had been infiltrated through and through, that they were completely powerless and had to be controlled from the outside.

Naturally, I was also to be subjected to gruelling scrutiny, and soon I was openly declared a collaborator who had been 'brought' into civil service under a secret mission to further India's objectives in Kashmir. The man who had met me at the university was now joined by many more with a similar opinion. The faint murmur became a deafening taunt. But I kept walking on the path I had chosen. Many well-wishers advised me that if I remained quiet this criticism might abate. But I didn't agree. I had seen even the quietest people losing their lives. So I continued talking about things around me. I had an opinion on what kind of future I wanted for my child, and I refused to be judged as someone on the wrong side of history.

In a place where narratives are fiercely contested, there will always be an attempt to prefer one victim and discredit the other. But while the victims of state-sanctioned violence have always found voices in their solidarity, the non-state victims have rarely seen any support. We are not here to talk about who killed how many. Counting dead bodies isn't the point. I have myself experienced how tragedies become cannon fodder for politics and how there are pro-state and anti-state forces battling it out to undermine some tragedies and overplay others. In Kashmir, the problem so far has been that while the state's action against innocents is often censured, there is a lot of innocent blood on invisible hands that no one talks about. Not only that, the tacit understanding is that the stories in which the state is not the villain are stories inimical to the reputation of the movement and these stories should not be told at all. Whenever there is a civilian killing and if the state is not the immediate suspect, there is silence and the benefit of the doubt invariably goes to the other side. No one understands that while a soldier's bullet only snuffs out the life, a militant's bullet slurs the soul too. It makes an *ikhwani* (pro-government militia) out of an innocent fence sitter. The responses are so glaringly different. The first one is oppression. The second one is a mistake. The first one deserves quick condemnation. The second one calls for compromise. The first one demands inquiry. The second one is a fait accompli. The former asks for revenge and the latter requires forbearance. It is this selective outrage and justification of one type of violence and condemnation of the other, rather than treating violence as inherently odious, which is one of the biggest evils of our political history so far.

Kashmir is a colossal tragedy and we need to look at it from the perspective of pain. Only those who have lost their dear ones in the last three decades can understand what absence of peace means. The first right to have an opinion on the Kashmir conflict is of those mothers who lost their sons in this bloody war, those women whose husbands left for the evening prayer and never returned, those Pandits who got deracinated, those children who grew up in the midst of war and lost their childhoods. An orphan is an orphan, whether the father fought for or against the state. A widow is a widow, whether the husband was killed in custody or killed in combat. A dead son is a hole in the heart, whether the son died defending one ideology or another. Only the victims of war know how important it is to end the war. Today all voices that call for an immediate end to all sorts of violence in Kashmir are berated as being statist and 'status-quoist' mainly by those who see a career in the perpetuation of this tragedy. Kashmir is one of the biggest intellectual hijacks of our times where those who have nothing to lose speak on behalf of those who have lost everything. This moral hazard where a few hatemongers argue for the continuation of violence to the detriment of those who are not their own flesh and blood is too obvious to be overlooked.

Six years after my selection and around three decades after the election that is often marked as a watershed in Kashmir's history for serving as a provocation for the onset of militancy, in 2016, we again witnessed the familiar replay of street power and state power pitched against each other—new memorials of violence created, new stories of victimhood and new tales added to the thriving narratives of loss around Kashmir. The loss of human life on both sides of the political divide has been agonizing and there has been immense outrage against the pellet guns in all sections of the society. But as I write this, and while the tail of the storm seems to have blown over, voices that are otherwise criticized for being pacifist and statist have again begun to gain relevance and people have started talking about alternatives to violence as a principal technique of grievance redressal. The problem so far has been that anything that was not entirely compliant with the dominant discourse was rubbished as being 'agency-talk'. But the biggest takeaway from this recent paroxysm of public anger has been that people have realized that discipline, non-violence and inclusiveness will have to be accepted as mainstream strategies to reach a resolution. No doubt the initiative has to come from the state but then the people also have to reciprocate in due measure.

My father would often tell me that a movement that is based on truth and has beauty as its goal will still have to ensure that its means are fair and just. Truth, beauty and justice have to go together. Today, while things are being discussed more openly, there is a call for introspection, victims are being counted irrespective of whose victims they are, rigid ideological positions are softening, an internal dialogue and debate has set in, positive stories are being shared and, after a phase of shouting and yelling, a phase of listening and self-reflection has set in. No story should be seen as defamatory of the Kashmir problem and that is how narratives will mature. Son of a deceased militant, widow of a killed soldier, daughter of a slaughtered civilian, a pellet victim, an injured police constable, a child who was brought up in exile—everyone's story must move us equally. There was a huge debate on celebration of achievers recently. It began with the emergence of 'too' many young Kashmiri champions and the consequent dismissal of this phenomenon as being state sponsored. Then it led to a feeling of self-injury and again there was a consensus that we need to celebrate our achievers. In a conflict zone even the most innocuous phenomena can generate very interesting dialectics—celebration, condemnation, self-introspection, escape; celebration being one set of such responses that I have personally experienced very closely. This should be seen as a very natural thing to happen.

I keep asking myself if there is any hope for Kashmir. I look at the divisions within, the unabated loss of life and limb, the youth bulge, the possessiveness about certain narratives, the absence of self-critical leadership, the intellectual vacuum, the disconnect with world politics and the reluctance to look for alternative strategies, and I feel very sad that one day my grandchildren might also have to listen to the advice that if you want to be safe in Kashmir you should keep silent. I am scared of a muted, mirthless future where death is celebrated and life is not. I look at the changing face of India and keep reassuring myself that this nation will not renege on the promise of democracy and secularism made in the preamble to its Constitution. And then I look at our own history, the great intellectual and political churning that we have experienced in the past, the rollercoaster of five millennia that went behind the formation of the Kashmiri identity, and I feel confident that we shall bounce back one day. We will keep arguing but we won't stop talking to one another. That has been the tradition. Kashmiris have gone through the worst. It can only get better now.

As a postscript to this essay, I am adding the story of a cat that lived in Shaf Tothas's attic. He would often tell me that he wanted to get rid of it as the feline would sniff at his sun-dried herbal medicines and then his clients would refuse to buy them. People here believe that if you eat something touched by a cat, it causes memory loss. Totally exasperated, one day he caught hold of it, cut a window in a polybag, tucked its head into it and carried it away to Kalaroos, a village around ten miles away. He left the cat there and returned home after a week, relieved that the nuisance was over. But he soon found out that the stubborn cat had reached home long before him and had munched on all the vitality herbs hanging over the eaves by then. In Kashmir, conflict has become like a cat in our attic. We don't want it yet we are not sure how to put an end to this company. The time has come to reflect upon the agony of lost decades; about hugging and forgiving one another and walking across the inner fault lines; talking to one another, rebuilding the lost trust, being proud of ourselves and celebrating our achievers, and bidding an imaginative farewell to arms. Non-violence has been our creed. And non-violence doesn't mean compromising on the pursuit of genuine political aspirations.

The Coma of Civilization

RAHUL PANDITA

Rahul Pandita is a journalist and the author of, among others, *Our Moon Has Blood Clots: A Memoir of a Lost Home in Kashmir*. He is a 2015 Yale World Fellow.

The first time I took the highway out of home, I was four years old. On the map, the land where I was born looked like the ideograph of a heart with an enlarged upper left chamber. After the first war, the upper chambers had disappeared; now it looked like a piece of bread baked by an amateur baker. But on the maps here, the land was still depicted in its pre-war form, as if that would result in some magical accretion of its geography.

When I travelled in a black Ambassador car to mainland India, I had no idea about my land's history. It was only in 1990, ten years after that first outward journey, that I realized how critically important knowing one's history was. It was the year my family and tens of thousands of others were hounded out of the land where our ancestors had lived for hundreds of decades. The exodus in 1990 was not the first one my people had faced; it had happened several times during invasions and conquests that began 700 years ago. At the time of my exile, though, I was ignorant about how much we had suffered for our gods and for nurturing the idea of a civilization.

But I vividly remember that journey I had taken at the age of four. I had pressurized my father into taking me along; he was going on an official trip with two of his colleagues. He was probably in his mid-thirties then. I remember he had said that he would get me gifts if I would let him go alone. But I had clung on, and he had finally given up.

The Ambassador car had passed through the saffron fields of Pampore and, by the roadside, stacks of willow clefts used for making cricket bats. Afterwards, we had crossed the tunnel that connected us to the rest of the country. The journey had become quite arduous as the car snaked through the Pir Panjal mountain range. I had watched with dread the sight of a truck turned into pulp by a giant boulder that had fallen over it at a place aptly named *khooni nala*, the killer rivulet.

By early evening, we had reached Jammu, our first vision of the Indian plains. People quite distinct from us lived here; they spoke a different language and we felt disassociated from their habits of food and everyday life. However, they worshipped the same gods as we did. At four, neither the difference in our language nor the commonality of our gods mattered. Nevertheless, after a few years, when I gradually became conscious of my religious identity, I began to take solace in the marches taken out there on Basant Panchami, in which our gods would be invoked. Jammu, in that sense, began to hold the promise of India—Hindu India—which to us then meant a place where we would not be in a minority and where nobody would mount an assault on our gods.

Back home, our idea of India was limited to certain imagery. Our foremost connection to the mainland was a man whose forefathers had taken the same highway at some point in the 700 years to escape religious persecution. On my sister's textbook, I saw a picture of him holding a hat in Cambridge and remember feeling an inexplicable pride when an uncle remarked that his nose resembled mine. That man had become the first prime minister of India or 'Barat' (which many years later I realized was to be pronounced 'Bharat') or Hindustan, which Iqbal told us was better than the entire world.

What other connections were there? We had a fondness for Swami Vivekananda, who had taken America by storm and who had visited my land, spending time at the goddess's shrine in my ancestral village. Then there was Adi Shankaracharya who had a temple named after him on a hill in the heart of Srinagar, and who, I was gleefully told by my elders, had lost a philosophical debate with a housewife of my land.

The kitschy connections were provided by actors from Bombay who pretended to row shikaras in the lake by the Mughal gardens and who chased their lovers on bicycles on roads lined with poplar trees; and by cricketers, whose pictures from *Sportstar* my college-going cousin pasted all over his room.

In the summer, hordes of tourists came as well. They would stay in hotels and in houseboats, and we would see them roaming around in the main city square named out of some Bolshevik sentiment as Lal Chowk, the red square. The summers also brought sadhus and labourers and beggars from the mainland. One woman, who had a soulful voice, sought alms at the main bus stand in Srinagar, singing a Hindi film song, '*Guzra hua zamana, aata nahi dobara, haafiz khuda tumhara* [The time which has passed away won't come back, may god be your protector]'.

In the humdrum of life, in almond blossoms and avalanches of snow, in our feasts and festivals, we somehow forgot the wounds of history. The ruins of the Martand Sun Temple in south Kashmir or the large ochre mark on the wall behind the Shah Hamadan Mosque between the third and fourth bridge over the Jhelum found no mention in our discourses. As a young boy, I once witnessed in my neighbourhood the razing of a temple that some people from my community were trying to build close to our street. It was seen as a sign of assertion; in no time, the old hostilities came alive and the wooden structure of the temple was brought down with the force of kicks.

I was very disturbed at the sight of the broken temple; I did not have a template then to understand invasions and conquests, but I saw in those broken wooden planks an acceptance of defeat. In that anguish, I went to my grandfather's brother. He listened to me patiently; then he quoted an experience shared by Swami Vivekananda with one of his disciples after he returned from the goddess's temple. The Swami was disturbed after looking at the ruins of temples destroyed by invaders. At this point, he had a vision of the goddess who told him: 'It is my desire that I should live in a dilapidated temple, otherwise can I not immediately erect a seven-storeyed temple of gold here if I like? What can you do? Shall I protect you or shall you protect me?'

Was it a correct vision? Or was it rather symptomatic of the civilizational coma that India had slipped into, which the writer V.S. Naipaul refers to in *India: A Wounded Civilization*:

Out of a superficial reading of the past, out of the sentimental conviction that India is eternal and forever revives, there comes not a fear of further defeat and destruction, but an indifference to it. India will somehow look after itself; the individual is free of responsibility.

When a few people brought down a wooden structure with a certain god inside, what victory did they achieve and against whom? When our neighbours and schoolmates sometimes called us *daali'e batta*—the dal-eating Pandits—were they attacking us (people who hardly consumed dal) or the connections between what they believed were a dal-eating people and the idea of a civilization? If my land was a part of India, then why did some people address the tourists from the mainland and ask them: 'Have you come from India?' As if in their minds, the mainland was some phantom limb severed from us long ago.

Back then we had no answers. In school, while we read about Mahatma Gandhi and the freedom struggle, the textbooks didn't tell us anything about our own history. The fifteenth-century historian, Jonaraja, who had traced the arc of the sword to our necks, was just a man who had written the *Dvitiya Rajatarangini*. During field trips to the museum, nobody told us the meanings of the idols and the artefacts. I don't think even the teachers had any clue about what they meant.

We might have had an indifference to Jonaraja and the tales of conquest and defeat he preserved for us, but there was one recent event of history whose lacerations were quite intact on our psyche. In October 1947, tribesmen from the North-West Frontier Province, aided by the state of Pakistan, attacked Kashmir and indulged in large-scale loot and plunder, and rape and killings. We called it *Kabai'el Raid*, the raid of the tribesmen. A friend's grandfather who had witnessed the horrors of the Partition in Punjab and had never spoken about it suddenly began to talk about it feverishly in his last days. He kept muttering, '*Tik pae gayi* [The attack has happened]'. The raid was to us what the '*tik*' was to the old man. Even seventy years later, we use 'raid' as a metaphor to describe any catastrophe.

It was the newly independent India that had sent its army to our rescue in 1947. As the raiders were pushed back, our fate with India was sealed. To us, India had saved much more than territory. It had saved a slice of civilization, without which its own history would be so incomplete and without any mooring.

For the Indians, Naipaul had said, the world was divided into India and non-India. For us, India was divided into Kashmir and non-Kashmir. It was evident in the rituals we followed, the almanac that guided our lives, the food we consumed and the *leelas* we sang for our gods. But we fiercely guarded our Indianness. We felt extreme pride at the sight of soldiers in their uniforms, marching down the Rajpath. It brought us solace that we are now protected and no invader could conquer us. In school, we sang the national anthem with passion, often braving kicks from others, who again saw it as a connection they badly wanted severed.

That our fate was tied to developments in the mainland became clear to me in June 1984. In Amritsar, Punjab, Indira Gandhi had decided to fight the demons she had created herself. The army had been called in to flush out extremists from the

Golden Temple, led by a man who had proclaimed himself a saint. As the operation was under way, a mob attacked the Hanuman Temple in Srinagar and threw the main idol in the Jhelum waters. Why would they do it? How could this be a response to something that had happened hundreds of miles away and in which we had no role to play?

By 1986, this hostility had become very visible. It is the year when riots broke out in south Kashmir; in the pre-social media era, we heard terrible stories of rape and plunder from friends and relatives. By 1989, this hostility had reached a crescendo. That winter we would venture out of our homes to find 'Indian dogs go back' scribbled on the walls on the streets. On the night of 19 January 1990, thousands of people assembled in mosques all over Kashmir and said they wanted to turn Kashmir into Pakistan—without the Pandit men, but with their women. To many who had cared to read history, the night brought back visions of the Afghan rule in Kashmir in the eighteenth century when hapless Pandits would be tied up in grass sacks and pushed into the Dal Lake.

The exodus began from the next day onwards.

In February 1990, it became impossible for us to celebrate Shivratri; as the ritual demanded, we took the gods to the riverside, but abandoned the celebratory conch, instead reciting ancient hymns under our breath. We felt choked and were brought to tears remembering our people who had been killed on the roads with a macabre dance performed around their corpses.

In the April of that year, my family took a taxi to escape to Jammu. We thought we were leaving for a short time; we thought things would become normal again for us to return like our forefathers had done several times in the past; we thought we would be able to take our gods to familiar waters and then celebrate the oncoming spring.

In Jammu, we felt relieved for a while. Here, we did not have to live in fear; we could worship our gods freely and recite our hymns loudly. We were not in Kashmir; we were in non-Kashmir. But it was still India, our India.

* * *

In the heart of Jammu, the refugees met every day in a compound of a temple. It is here that the magnitude of ancient hatred became clear to us. From one corner of our land to another, the Pandits had been brutalized.

A professor who was a Marxist and spent a lot of time at the coffee house in Srinagar missed his conversations a lot. He was not ignorant about history but had viewed it from such a distance that it had left him untouched. While leaving home, he had been jeered at by a mob in his neighbourhood; they had thrown candy at him the way one did with the dead. But even in the clarity of that candy shower, he had been in a sort of disbelief. In that temple compound, surrounded by a dejected mass, he was taken over by the spirit of history; it also made him hopeful about the Indian state. In a fervent voice, he declared that the nation was not going to take our exodus lightly. He predicted that there would be such massive protests at the Boat Club in Delhi that the Parliament would come to a halt. He said he was certain that 'our own people' would open their homes to us.

But none of this really happened. In refugee camps, which were set up in Jammu and elsewhere, we were given biscuits and blankets, but not the balm of oneness that the professor had predicted would be offered to us. It was as if with a little relief of food and bedding alone, the equilibrium of dharma would be restored. In only a few days, in the Hindu Jammu, we realized that a landlord is neither Hindu nor Muslim—he is just a mercenary for profit.

Days would turn into weeks, and weeks would turn into months and years, but we would never return. In narratives spun by journalists and academics and activists and leading lights of civil liberties, our story did not even find mention in a footnote. There was 1984; then there was 1992; and then there was 2002. The events of 1992 and 2002 had resulted in an array of protests, essays, plays, movies and black armbands. In public meetings, I would sometimes walk in like a trapeze artiste and throw in my gauntlet.

'Kashmir, Sirs?'

'Ah, Kashmir! Terrible. Barbed wire. Rum-eyed soldiers.'

'Kashmiri Pandits?'

'Ah, well. They were elites. They became collateral damage in revolution. Our sympathies are with them, but these things happen.'

In the 1990s, a political party chose to make our story theirs. To make that happen, it pulled out, like a rabbit from a magician's hat, Syama Prasad Mookerjee, their Nehru equivalent—a man who had been stopped at the border of Jammu and Kashmir in 1953 and then taken to Srinagar, where he died in detention in rather mysterious circumstances. In 1992, the party leadership invoked his name, and 50,000

51

people landed up in Jammu. Led by a senior leader and one of his bearded deputies, they said they would go to Srinagar and unfurl the national flag at Lal Chowk. We were told that it was intended to fill the chasm, which radical separatists had created between Kashmir and India.

From inside the buses, the supporters shouted slogans of '*Jahan hue balidan Mookerjee, woh Kashmir humara hai* [The Kashmir where Mookerjee was martyred is ours].' I remember asking people in crumpled clothes and sadhus holding replicas of tridents in their hands about Mookerjee. They knew nothing about the man.

In the end, only seventy people made it to Lal Chowk under heavy security. The unfurling of the national flag turned into a spectacle. The pole of the flag snapped in the middle and the bearded deputy had to tie it with a handkerchief to keep it erect.

That pole is yet to be mended. Almost three decades have passed and the chasm seems to be wider than ever. And even today, as it was then, the custodians of secularism keep on inventing false analogies to whitewash our ethnic cleansing. The word 'Kashmiriyat'—used to indicate a sort of syncretism—pushed down our throats as if it were some sweet pill intended to soothe our throats is hemlock to us. Our story continues to be told in scare quotes, which, as the philosopher Susan Neiman puts it, 'expresses the speaker's discomfort in the ultimate postmodern gesture'.

In exile, the Marxist professor got dejected with his false heroes. He began to visit temples, which he had never done before.

In the refugee camp once, a European delegation came to pay a visit. An old man insisted that he be allowed to speak to the head of the delegation. The man began his story from Sikandar 'Butshikan', the fourteenth-century iconoclast who broke the Sun Temple; by the time he touched upon the recent developments, the westerner had become too confused. 'So, Sikandaar Botchicken is a commander of Hizbul Mujahideen?' he asked. At which point, the old man became silent. Everyone around him became silent.

It was not the old man's failure; it was the failure of a civilization. He must have felt so helpless in front of a foreigner. His own people, his own leaders had failed him miserably. It was as if the incident had only proven Naipaul's point when he wondered whether intellectually for a 1000 years, India hadn't always retreated before its conquerors and whether, in its periods of apparent revival, India hadn't only been making itself archaic again, intellectually smaller, always vulnerable.

* * *

The city of Jammu suffocated me. To me, it became a reminder of what we had lost. Two decades ago, I came to Delhi and it is where I continue to live. My restlessness took me to other places; it took me to Bastar where I witnessed a different war.

One day, while travelling with a squad of Maoist guerrillas through a dense forest in the night, I was led inside a small hut in the middle of nowhere. As I entered, I saw that an Adivasi man and his wife were about to have food: a plate of rice, more stones than grain. They had lit a small fire. As we sat, I noticed that the man was weeping. I asked the Maoist commander to ask him why he was crying. He replied that he just felt like crying.

How would one put this sentiment in words? What did that man go through? What hatred, ancient or modern, had he witnessed?

We spent the night in that hut and continued our onward journey before sunrise. When we left, the man was not there. In my heart I knew that I would never meet him again.

In the jungle, while I was alone, I often thought of my own home and the lost gods. In the villages, the Adivasis would, after a person's death, put all his personal belongings by his grave. It was as if they had easiness with death, which sadly the state would not let them have with life. And now the revolutionaries, who claimed to be fighting for them, were slitting their throats as well. I kept writing about it; my writings were mostly about the plight of the Adivasis and how they were caught in the war between the state and the Maoist guerrillas. But many thought I was sympathetic to the guerrillas, whom they saw as a threat to the construct of India. Some of them, who knew my history of exile, began to call me *dhimmi*, a person who is granted special status in Muslim lands in return for paying a certain tax (in my case the tax being the sympathy they thought I displayed for certain narratives).

In a city, I met a former Maoist who had left the party after falling in love. He had promised his wife that he would never indulge in violence again. The man was a Dalit and lived with his wife in a *basti*. Whenever I went to meet my friend there, I would always feel as if its narrow streets were laden with centuries of anger. But unlike heaps of garbage, this anger was invisible; it was there in a very profound way and manifested fissure-like in the behaviour of its inhabitants.

One day, my friend came to my hotel room. We had plans to drink together. I had bought a bottle of whisky earlier. It was very hot and, as I entered the bathroom to take a shower, my friend went out to get a snack. He returned in a few minutes. As I finished my bath, I realized that I had forgotten my clothes outside. I would have to come out wrapped in a towel. That was okay, there was no formality between us. However, I felt stranded in the bathroom because of a major indecision. I was wearing my *janeu*, the sacred thread that I wore because it made me feel connected to my roots. But to the man outside, it meant something else. It is not as if he did not know that I was a Brahmin. I remembered a previous evening when my friend had got very emotional. He had said he felt sorry sometimes that he had to leave the Maoist movement and that people like me, privileged (he did not use that word but implied it), were willing to put up more fight against the state than him.

And now, the act of wearing the thread would make me a non-revolutionary in his eyes.

In the summer heat, I broke into a sweat as I stood inside the bathroom for several minutes, debating with myself whether to come out like this or remove the thread. I finally decided to keep it on and come out.

That evening, something changed between us. I did not see how my friend reacted when I came out like that, as my back was turned towards him. Afterwards, we just sat and had a few drinks with the little snack. We talked as well, but the grain of that conversation had changed. And I knew it had altered permanently.

Even as I met the leaders of the movement, in jungles and in their small living rooms in university campuses, there was a discomfort that remained between us. In the beginning, I never figured out why it was so. But gradually I understood. They expected me to not only shun my belief system but also to abuse it. I worked very hard and reported from guerrilla zones, bringing to the fore stories of the void left by the state. It suited the movement well. But then, they wanted to decide my political commitments for me so that they could claim my stories as their own. They did not have the vision to realize that while we might share certain common ground, my belief system could be different from theirs. They were unhappy, for example, that I was not peddling their narrative on Kashmir. They were unhappy that I would not support an old separatist leader from Kashmir who had publicly said that he had no belief in democracy or the idea of India, and that by virtue of Islam, Kashmir was a part of Pakistan. I could not forget that the man belonged to a party that would slaughter cows on Janmashtami just to antagonize us.

With the same duplicitous zeal they built up false narratives in universities. They lacked moral clarity and did not find it odd that even on fixed parameters their concept of social justice was arbitrary. They refused to see beyond the parentheses of their vision. With their churlish festivals and derogatory retelling of stories sacred to many of us, they pushed a mass of people to the margins. But they forgot that India was a wounded civilization.

It might not have the intellectual means to move ahead, as Naipaul felt, but many had their own ideas of addressing their inadequacies.

One of them was to vote for that bearded leader who had used his handkerchief to keep the pole intact in Lal Chowk. That man is now the prime minister of India.

We are still in exile. But for those who addressed the inadequacies of a wounded civilization by voting for a certain man, it was just a way they thought the equilibrium of dharma could be restored.

The (In)Dignity of Our Sexualities

GAUTAM BHAN

Gautam Bhan teaches at the Indian Institute for Human Settlements, Bengaluru, where his work focuses on urban poverty, inequality and welfare. He has been part of social movements on gender and sexuality rights in Delhi for many years. He is the author of *In the Public's Interest: Evictions, Citizenship and Inequality in Contemporary Delhi*, as well as the co-editor of *Because I have a Voice: Queer Politics in India*.

There are many lines you can read again and again from the 2009 Delhi High Court judgment—commonly known as the Naz case—that decriminalized same-sex sexual relations in India. Let me give you one that has stayed with me since that day in the courtroom:

> For every individual, whether homosexual or not, the sense of gender and sexual orientation of the person are so embedded . . . that the individual carries this aspect of his or her identity wherever he or she goes. While recognizing the unique worth of each person, the Constitution does not presuppose that the holder of rights is an isolated, lonely and abstract figure possessing a disembodied and socially disconnected self. It acknowledges that people live in their bodies, their communities, their cultures, their places and their times.[1]

---

[1] Naz Foundation vs National Capital Territory of Delhi WP(C) No.7455/2001.

Bodies, communities, cultures, places and times. In one sentence, the judges reminded us of what we talk about when we talk about sexuality. Not just sexual orientation or gender identity, meant to be only about some people who are lesbian, gay, bisexual or transgender. Not just something called 'gay rights', somehow separated from other intrinsic rights and freedoms. Not even just individual lives lived as if they could exist on islands of freedom.

When they spoke of sexuality, the judges spoke of more than this. They spoke of sexuality as an intimacy both public and private, something we individually possessed but whose life was stitched into what we made together: families, communities, cities, nations. Sexuality as being not just about sex, body, identity and desire, but equally about politics and democracy. Sexuality, they reminded us, can be a powerful litmus test for the possibility of dignity within a constitutional democracy.

As a gay man, this is what I read and heard in Naz: the possibility of, and insistence on, dignity. Sexuality as dignity becomes something else in our hands. It becomes not just about a life free of violence but one of personhood, even of joy. It imagines bodies not just tolerated but loved and desired by ourselves and by others. It speaks of rights not just possessed but practised. It holds choices of ways to live lives that are not just possible but meaningful and feasible, without needing extraordinary courage or immense privilege. It draws spaces from our homes to the public spaces of our cities that can invite and embrace our presence.

When sexuality comes with dignity, we don't hold our breath so often, whether in fear or regret.

As India turns seventy, what can we say about the possibilities of dignity within our sexualities? In this essay, I offer just two of the many stories one can tell of sexuality in contemporary India. The first is the story of the legal challenge to Section 377 of the Indian Penal Code, an 1861 Victorian-era law that criminalized 'voluntary carnal intercourse against the order of nature' and acted, effectively, as an anti-sodomy statute. The second is a rumination on the Indian city to see what kind of places it offers sexuality, how it holds it, and what it tells us about the possibilities of dignity. These are stories that are both intertwined and distinct, seemingly unconnected but, I will argue, actually deeply imbricated in each other with much to offer us in terms of reading the nation in what seems like another moment of transition and churning.

Moving, Perhaps Forward

In 2015, a student at the Indian Institute of Science (IISc) in Bengaluru was blackmailed and threatened with being publicly exposed for being gay. When he refused to pay extortion money, the private letters turned into notices pinned on noticeboards on campus. The words were sharp, relentless and inhumane: 'I think it's completely shameful, bad, immoral and disgusting. You should go kill yourself. Why do you think it's illegal to be gay in India?'

For many queer people, this moment is familiar. It is one that many of us have faced or live in constant fear of facing. In some ways, it is the latter that is worse. We live our lives anticipating prejudice. Even before it comes, we are constantly censoring, moving and shaping our lives to evade it or, if we can't, survive it. Those of us who have the privilege of privacy, scan rooms to find allies, weigh what to tell our doctors, measure out information in our offices and seek safe spaces. Those without this privilege face a much more direct battle to be who they are: an unrelenting and legitimized public violence that falls on working-class bodies in our streets, police stations and public spaces. The law is not the only force behind this violence, but it is an important one. 'Why do you think,' the blackmailer asks, 'it's illegal to be gay in India?' When petitioners in the Naz argued that Section 377 of the Indian Penal Code played an important part in shrouding our lives in criminality and legitimizing violence, this letter was one of many that we wrote against in our heads.

In 2009, Naz gave many of us—not all, never all, for the law does not have such power by itself—a feeling of complete personhood. This was not just because of the judgment in itself but also because of the kind of judgment it was, the modes of argument, the language it gave us. The judges sought to use the law to build a space around our lives that would embrace, protect, nurture and even love queer people. They never spoke of tolerance. They imagined law at its best, its highest form, as an instrument that would not just protect difference but value it. When they asked us to embrace our 'constitutional morality'— our morality as citizens, not as individuals—they gave us a way to be democratic, to separate our personal beliefs and our faith from our duties as citizens in a plural, open world. Naz was never just a judgment on gay rights: it was a judgment on dignity, on the possibility of social as well as political equality.

In December 2013, a two-judge bench of the Supreme Court overturned Naz. On that day, I remember, it had simply felt difficult to breathe. Naz had seemed to mark a threshold of some kind. Queer struggles had always been much more than the law and more than just one law in particular. Yet, as the battles that had led up to 2009 spilled outward as the judgment's words travelled outside and beyond the courtroom, it felt impossible to believe that after this one could move—even though hesitantly—anyway but forward. That morning, no other verdict seemed possible. It was. Only one summary sentence was read out and a two-judge Supreme Court bench overturned Naz.[2]

So what does it look like from within our fears? What has happened since the Supreme Court reversal of Naz? In one sense, it has been extraordinary. The reversal drew widespread condemnation in different forms and sites, from an extraordinary range of voices. The then-ruling government, led by the Indian National Congress, came out for the first time in strong and public support of queer rights as did several other parties including the Communist Party of India (Marxist), the Janata Dal (S) and the Aam Aadmi Party. Several parties endorsed sexuality rights in their election manifestos for the 2014 general election, making queer rights a part of every election debate. At the time of the judgment, the attorney general wrote an unprecedented opinion piece in a leading newspaper against the judgment and filed a review petition immediately. Suddenly,

---

[2] Suresh Kumar Koushal vs Naz Foundation Civil Appeal 10972 of 2013, also recorded as SLP 15436 of 2009.

politics of the party kind became a new battleground for queer rights—something the movement had evaded until now, certain that there was little support to be found. However, another powerful national party—the Bharatiya Janata Party (BJP)—remained steadfast in opposition, and many significant regional parties remained silent.

Yet, it was the support in everyday life that began to show many of us that something had shifted between 2001 when the Naz Foundation filed the petition, 2005 when Voices Against 377 intervened in the case, 2009 when the Delhi High Court ruled and 11 December 2013. The sense in the days post the judgment has been one where a sea of voices has risen against the Supreme Court. One set comes from a generation of urban young people who have come of age in a post-2009 world, a set of political subjects in one sense created by the queer movement of the past decade.

What's important and a reflection of the movement itself is that the support has come not just from queer people, but across a range of actors, movements and institutions, many of whom had been hesitant friends in the early days of the movement. Progressive groups, state bodies like the National Human Rights Commission, teachers' associations, professional associations including the medical and mental health establishments, women's groups, student groups, trade unionists and private companies came out publicly against the judgment. Thousands across the country stood together, repeating the chant that brought together our resistance: 'No Going Back.' A week after the judgment, 'No Going Back' protests to mark a 'Global Day of Rage' took place across thirty-six cities in the world, including seventeen in India. That resistance remains amidst the uncertainty and the fear, unwavering, unafraid. It is that resistance that stands as the legacy of December 2013.

After what should have been a moment of dismissal and closure turned into a moment of beginning, defiance and resistance, I want to believe that efforts to not let the queer movement be reduced to just a legal case against Section 377 have, if only partially, succeeded. The legal journey of the movement looms large at this moment, but the everyday life of our politics has always been about much more—even if the story of that larger politics is less told. Film festivals, workshops, talks and seminars; books, pamphlets, missives, poems, biographies, charters, manifestos; political visions, solidarities with other struggles, protests, pride parades; the creation of social spaces; facing, countering and recovering from acts of violence, blackmail, rape, assault and suicide; engaging with the police, with families, with religious leaders; the judiciary, the state; living open, everyday lives despite the odds, despite the pushback, refusing to stay 'private', to stay silent—the 2009 judgment was born not just out of the letter of the law but from this politics that had paved the way for it, that made it possible.

For me, *this* is—the struggle to change the language and life of sexuality—the legacy of the fight against Section 377. It is not the court case, either in its victory or in its defeat. The communities, cultures and places that Naz reminded us we inhabit are not determined or governed by law alone, just as the victories in law are not made in the courtroom alone. Knowing this, recognizing it, is pivotal.

In February 2016, the Supreme Court once again churned, agreeing in an extraordinary move to reopen Naz. A constitutional bench will now hear a curative petition to decide on the way forward. The legal battle stands reinstated. Yet, regardless of what happens in court, what remains just as true is this: with or without the law, the IISc student wrote back. He pinned a reply on the same noticeboard and spoke about not being ashamed of his sexuality. He reminded us that slowly, even if still incompletely, queer people have begun to win the greatest battle of our lives: we have begun to believe that we have the right to have rights. We have begun to believe that we have the right to dignity, the right to our bodies, the right to be happy. Whether these rights come through law or through struggle, they will come. In a moment, where there are so many who are made to believe that they are redundant and negligible, the value of this cannot be underestimated. You cannot blackmail someone—said the student in his reply pinned with a familiar golden thumb pin on the green felt of the noticeboard—who isn't ashamed.

Sexuality and the Indian City

I have often wondered what it was that encouraged that student to write back. Somewhere in that moment is a future, a mark of where we want to be. If Naz is right, if we are not disembodied selves, then none of our courage is just our own. It is the public in which we are embedded that makes courage ordinary rather than rare. In public spaces where the norm embraces differences, dignity will not feel like a test. It will not require extraordinary amounts of privilege or courage. For every queer person who writes back to his blackmailer, there are dozens who didn't, who won't, who can't. Our task is not just to celebrate the one who fought, but to create a scenario where the fight won't be necessary.

Here is where our second story comes up. One that remembers the other lessons from Section 377—the ones learnt outside the court. One that looks beyond the language of formal rights, institutions and the law. One that takes us back to sexuality in its public life, in the way it shapes the worlds we all must inhabit. The second story then is of one such site where many of us seek to make our lives: the city.

Cities, the story goes, are the roots of civitas and of demos. City, citizens, civility, civilization. Demos, democracy. They are where we come to be modern, cosmopolitan, open to dealing with difference. If sexuality is a test of dignity in our democracy, then our cities are one of its most important examination rooms and battlegrounds. They have been so, globally and in India, often. Let us not forget that Ambedkar rested his fate in the city, seeing it as a site where a new form of life that would shed caste could be possible. His faith is mirrored in much of our sense of urban life: its modes allow and are built on difference, its anonymity a protection. Cities belong to different publics, no single identity, no single way of life, no one sense of 'right' or 'wrong' can dominate a metropolis. It is in such a city that sexuality could, should, must be able to take its different paths, where it can reach for dignity rather than a bare life.

Today in India, our cities often seem silent in the face of this promise. They feel imperilled, distant from their own possibilities. Nowhere is this more evident than when one thinks of sexuality. It is fear, distance, prejudice and intolerance that seem to have dug themselves deeper, just as the institutions and democratic safeguards meant to combat these flounder. The ranks of urban residents who have experienced that deeply queer moment of exclusion and otherness, whether it speaks the particular idiom of sexuality or not, have grown. This matters deeply for sexuality. Queer politics has long insisted that it is not just about the rights of the LGBT people. It has insisted that our multiple identities cannot be pried apart from one another. We are not either Hindu or gay or transgender or Dalit or able or female; we are many or all of them at once. A city that cannot make space for difference and dissent will never be one where queer people can be safe, let alone possess dignity, or attain happiness. A city without a sense of the public—of a shared space, a sense of belonging across difference of all kinds—is and can only be a city of walls, gates and 'others'.

As I write, the streets of Lucknow are patrolled by anti-Romeo squads, seeking to punish love that they can only read in terms of jihad. Love that crosses caste, class or religion is routinely, violently and spectacularly punished. Difference is marked, berated, denied. Universities have become the sites of policing and moral, physical and sexual control. The bodies of African women and men have been brutalized, laid open to legitimized violence in both public and private. People from Manipur, Mizoram, Meghalaya and Nagaland have left Bengaluru in midnight trains. The everyday occurrence of sexual violence that women and transgendered people face remains so ordinary that it is often not even recognized as violence until it takes the form of spectacular assault, often death.

The list is endless. We appear to be in our cities, in this historical conjuncture, immeasurably far from dignity, from the possibility of joy. Our fights are still about the barest of life, the right to be free from direct physical violence, to simply be acknowledged, to have the possibility of an encounter unmarked by assumptions and prejudice, to not constantly be on guard, to not constantly hold our breath. Legally winning against Section 377 will just bring queer people into this fight, to have the right at least to begin to fight it—it can do no more.

Why are our cities like this? Behind the incidents of rupture that overcrowd our attention and our outrage, there are patterns. It is those that we need to begin to see. Our cities are deeply divided geographies. All have neighbourhoods, streets and buildings where only those of 'one kind' can live, some through power and others through powerlessness. In no Indian city can either law or norm prevent discrimination in being able to rent a house if you step an inch outside marriage, gender norms, religious differences or caste hierarchies. New forms of city-making seek enclosures, privatize space and create peripheries. Gates rather than streets mark our urban forms, creating spaces where people can only meet as fragments, as others.

Speech feels increasingly censored by force or fear, muzzling both dissent and desire. The political establishment narrows the imagination of what can be said or thought, using the idea of a 'people' to exclude rather than open; the imagination of a 'nation' to build borders instead of undoing them. A man who asked for the bodies of Muslim women to be exhumed and raped holds a high elected office, another who stood by their sexual and physical erasure holds one higher still. Marital rape remains legal. Sexual violence by the army still claims impunity. In Srinagar, Dantewada and Imphal, no one holds the right to their bodies at all, not even to basic life. Majoritarian power feels emboldened and entitled, the 'norm' not a way of life, but simply the way of life. More often than not, such majoritarian thought exercises its power precisely on the bodies, communities, cultures and places that Naz told us we belong to. What does it mean for queer people, any people, to have rights in a moment like this?

It is time we face the patterns of entrenched hierarchy, prejudice and intolerance that have taken hold in our cities. Urbanization has not brought—somehow magically by itself—new forms of social life. It will not until we begin to fight for a new kind of urbanism. Sexuality is never part of the usual discussions on what kind of cities we want. It should be. We will then understand why our newspaper headlines scream what they do, and why these headlines should not surprise us because they, in fact, reflect what we are, what we have let ourselves become.

For those who like to tell the stories through data, here are some. Across 2016–17, the Centre for the Study of Developing Societies (CSDS) surveyed—across the nation—young people aged between fifteen and thirty-four. What they found is the roots of the attitudes that result in the spectacular incidents that draw our outrage but cannot sustain the depths of our inquiry. The survey is stark. Only 4 per cent of young urban residents have married outside their caste. The urban retains caste endogamy, nearly seven decades after Ambedkar's warning. Nearly 41 per cent agree, in varying degrees, that married women should not work, and 51 per cent think wives should always listen to their husbands. Nearly 75 per cent disapprove of same-sex romantic relationships. For all the incidents we mentioned above, the roots are embedded: nearly 22 per cent express at least some unease about a neighbour from a different religion, 26 per cent about an African neighbour. Nearly half of respondents expressed concern about an unmarried boy and girl living together.

If sexuality is dignity, then its roots are in the quiet everyday of our lives. Once the difference between majority and other, normative and 'different' is drawn, the possibility of dignity fades. It will fade, often, into the violence that we can see but this violence is not an agent or an act, it is merely an inevitable outcome. When we look at our cities, we are reminded that these lines of differences are not just between LGBT and 'others'— difference disrespects such neat categories. It leaks into all our selves and our spaces, shapes the way we encounter and meet each other. It leaks into the possibilities of what we could become.

Where to from Here?

In his last speech to the Constituent Assembly, Ambedkar warned us that the political equality that our Constitution ensures would mean little if the social inequality that marked us was to remain unchanged. His words are well worth quoting at length:

On the 26th of January 1950, we are going to enter into a life of contradictions. In politics we will have equality and in social and economic life we will have inequality. In politics we will be recognizing the principle of one man one vote and one vote one value. In our social and economic life, we shall, by reason of our social and economic structure, continue to deny the principle of one man one value. How long shall we continue to live this life of contradictions? How long shall we continue to deny equality in our social and economic life?[3]

Today, both his diagnoses and warning feel apt and urgent. The contrasting tales in this essay can be interpreted as political and social equality being related but distinct fights. The fight against Section 377 will bring us more political equality. This is necessary, but not sufficient. The fight for sexuality as dignity cannot be won only through political equality in law and rights. The communities, cultures, places and times we inhabit are where differences take root. It is only in taking on these roots that we can move forward.

That the roots are intertwined is a truism that is both banal and critical. Our challenge is to find how to fight these roots together, to find ways to take on the entrenchment of difference as inequality and shift its narrative to difference as joy, plurality and multiplicity. I write today to urge us to take the city seriously as a battleground for this struggle, a critical one that will shape much of our futures. Ambedkar's hope was the cities

---

[3] Excerpts from Dr Ambedkar's speech to the Constituent Assembly, indexed in Constituent Assembly Debates, Vol. XI, 25 November 1949, http://164.100.47.132/LssNew/cadebatefiles/C23111949.pdf, accessed 6 May 2017.

that could hold the possibility for social equality. He was both right and wrong, but his hope must remain our own aspiration. We cannot cede our cities to an ordering of difference that falls too easily into prejudice, inequality and hierarchies. Doing so, however, means recognizing the terms of this fight. Not just outrage at an incident of sexual violence, not just speaking of LGBT people as if they alone embody sexuality, not pretending that other inequalities—on class, religion, caste and ability— can persist while sexuality somehow changes and morphs into its island of freedom.

The first step then is to recognize all the multiple fractures that break the bodies of our cities today. It is to step away from our self-congratulation on our gains in political equality to face the reality of the entrenchment and deepening of our social inequalities. The second, for those of us who wish to fight this fight from within sexuality, is to give ourselves new language for this fight, to begin seeing sexuality as a fight for dignity and personhood. The third is to grapple slowly, uncertainly and without any promises of easy wins to find ways to take on the differences between us. One way of moving forward that can hold both the needs and demands of social and political equality together is to frame our struggles for new laws and imaginations that protect different communities from discrimination. Anti-discrimination laws remain huge lacunae in our constitutional jurisprudence, and if the fight for them can create new openings that can begin to call out our existing cleavages, they may well be the first move in reimagining our differences.

Each of us will fight this fight in a different way—in our intimate lives, in our communities, in law, in our streets, in our own minds. All of these fights are needed; none of them alone will be enough. Yet, if sexuality can tell us one thing about India at seventy, it is that Ambedkar's fight still remains the battle of our time, and that it is high time that the fight for social equality finally found its place alongside, if not ahead of, political equality.

Through the Past into the Future

YASHWANT SINHA

Yashwant Sinha, former union finance minister and minister for external affairs, is a senior leader of the Bharatiya Janata Party. He is the author of *Confessions of a Swadeshi Reformer: My Years as Finance Minister* (Penguin, 2007).

When I think of India, I think of a country eternal—a country which has survived the onslaught of history and maintained its unique identity through the ages. Outsiders have invaded India for its wealth, conquered it, ruled it and have either been completely assimilated into it or have gone back.

When I think of India I think of a country, which is a strange amalgam of people living across vestiges of time even today. One just has to travel a short distance within the country to move from the present twenty-first century back to the fifth century BCE. If we grasp these two facts about India, we will be able to understand it better in all its myriad ways. India's accumulated history and its geographical spread spanning various climatic zones, makes it quite unique.

In an eternal country, things change but slowly. Revolutions of any kind and especially of the violent kind are rare and infrequent. We are more comfortable if things move at a gradual pace. The people are unhurried and prefer one step at a time rather than a leap forward. Most of us are generally self-centred, more concerned with the problems of our daily lives than the more momentous issues, national or international.

I cannot forget the experience recorded in his memoirs by the late Samir Ghosh, an IAS officer of the Bihar cadre. He was serving as a magistrate in Ranchi, then a part of Bihar. India was on its way to independence and 15 August was a momentous day in the history of our country. Ghosh was asked by his superiors to visit some villages in the district on that day and educate the people about the importance of a free India. He travelled from village to village for this purpose.

In one village, after he had finished explaining the importance of the day an innocent villager got up and asked him a simple question, 'When are we likely to get a fresh supply of kerosene oil?'

You talk to the people today and you will find that nothing really has changed in the last seventy years. Their concerns remain the same.

Paharia is a tribe, generally found in the old district of Santhal Pargana (now a zone of six districts in Jharkhand). It is a small tribe, almost on the point of extinction and lives only on mountaintops. They generally survive on forest produce and jhum (shifting) cultivation and therefore move from one range of hills to another.

When I was the deputy commissioner of Santhal Pargana in the late 1960s, I visited one of their habitations. My arrival was expected and the tribesmen who lived there had already gathered at one place to welcome me. Their headman addressed the gathering and said that they were happy that a representative of the 'Company Bahadur' had come to visit them after a long time. It took me a while to realize that he was actually referring to the East India Company. One hundred and ten years after the takeover by the British crown and twenty years after the independence of India, this tribe still lived in the distant past.

In my travels, on foot, to the various villages in Hazaribag district of Jharkhand, which is part of the Lok Sabha constituency of the same name, I have come across small tribal habitations where people live in the same way they would have lived perhaps in the centuries before Christ.

India has always been a nation, though the boundaries of the nation were not restricted within the confines of a single nation state until the British conquered and redefined India within the limited boundaries of a nation state. This concept of a nation state had emerged in Europe in the seventeenth and eighteenth centuries but was alien to India. India has always been a nation but not a nation state. Rather, it has been a collection of various sub-nationalities generally cohabiting in peace featuring sporadic bursts of violence.

We are still grappling with the problem of the accommodation of all our sub-nationalities within one nation state. It is perhaps this character of our nation, which has also led to our subjugation from time to time, often with the help of some disgruntled element or the other from within. The external invasions concerned only those who were directly attacked. They did not bother the others. Rarely was an invasion regarded as an invasion of the entire motherland. It is also the reason for the partition of India into various nation states today.

Matthew Arnold, the English poet, captured the character of India while describing the invasion of Alexander. He wrote,

'She (India) let the legions thunder past and plunged in thought again.'

Mahatma Gandhi also understood the character of India correctly when he decided to launch a non-violent struggle to achieve its independence. Nothing else would have succeeded. He knew that an armed struggle would be against the innate nature of the people and was unlikely to succeed. Non-violence, where you allow yourself to suffer, rather than imposing suffering on your adversary; where you allow yourself to get assaulted rather than assaulting your adversary; where you assert your moral authority rather than any other, was more suited to India's character. After all, the teachings of non-violence by our sages and seers through the ages have not gone in vain rather they have left a deep imprint on our psyche.

Gandhi's non-violence succeeded, secured us our independence and was adopted elsewhere in the world.

With non-violence comes the spirit of abnegation. In India, sacrifice is always a matter of great admiration; showing off your worldly possessions is not. The saint was always more revered than 'satta', the seat of temporal authority. No wonder then that Gandhi gave up all his clothes except the dhoti, and the dress code of the freedom fighters was the kurta and the pyjama or the dhoti. It represented simplicity and sacrifice. The leader could feel closer to the people in this attire rather than a three-piece suit. The dress code has survived in our politics to this day without the morality associated with the spirit of abnegation.

Indian politics and politicians have also undergone a radical change during the last seventy years after our independence.

The first governments at the Centre and in the states consisted of people who had made sacrifices, given up the comforts of life, fought for the freedom of the country and spent years in jail. They gave us our constitution, the institutions of democracy and the precedents and conventions to guide our public life. Ethics and morality played an important role. Elections were cheap, bicycles were used to campaign, and nights were spent not in five-star hotels but in voters' huts.

Power, however, can corrupt. Some in government succumbed to this temptation. The thugs and Pindaris forever present in our system took advantage of this weakness and did their best to make it more widespread and attractive. Winning elections and capturing power emerged as ends unto themselves so that the unscrupulous could take advantage of the system. The use of money power and muscle power with the help of unscrupulous businessmen and criminals emerged as the preferred tools to win elections. Booth capturing and other electoral malpractices followed.

The criminals and the businessmen, who helped others win elections, soon realized that they could themselves win polls. While the number of businessmen contesting elections remained limited, the number of criminals contesting elections increased by leaps and bounds. Criminalization of politics soon followed and the entire democratic system was compromised. Corruption in government became the rule rather than the exception. Politicians became the subject of hate and ridicule in society but very few people came forward to remedy the ailment. Politics indeed became the last refuge of the*********. Elections generally stopped reflecting the will of the people.

Fortunately, while the politicians lagged behind for their own selfish reasons, the Election Commission of India took the lead and started to reform the electoral system, especially when T.N. Seshan was the chief election commissioner. The people followed, though the political parties were reluctant. Today, I can say with a degree of confidence that things are not as bad as they were some years ago. A lot, however, remains to be done to restore the purity and the credibility of the electoral system, the parliamentary system and the institutions of democracy.

Executive despotism is not unknown even in the best of democracies. Despite the checks and balances provided in the Constitution, it is not difficult for a democratically elected leader to subvert them and become a despot. One does not have to declare an emergency, as Indira Gandhi had to do in 1975, to exercise absolute power and control the life of the citizen. In the post-truth age, with the army of trolls at the disposal of those who can afford them, truth is what is purveyed. The social media has truly become antisocial and lies are spread with a vengeance. I am sure all of us have interesting stories to tell about the untruths we have been subjected to by those trolls. Means of communication have expanded at a scorching pace; they have become as fast as light and have pervaded every living space. We believe what we hear and see. What we hear and see is what is dished out to us.

The media, whose responsibility it is to bring correct and truthful information to the people is, it seems more often than not, largely compromised because it has become overtly commercial. Its profits are more important for a media house than truth, and profits will depend on being on the right side of the government of the day.

The corporate houses, which own the media houses, are still dependent on the government for their prosperity and profitability. Paid news has emerged as a new curse for our democracy. Profits for the media houses and power for the politician have become the new creed.

When I was contesting the Lok Sabha elections in 2009 a local TV channel approached me with the suggestion that they would influence the voters by projecting me in a good light provided I agreed to pay them a specified large sum of money. I refused. The result was that the channel went hammer and tongs against me and did it so viciously that people stopped believing it; I received a lot of unpaid publicity and won the election. But my complaint to the Election Commission did not produce any outcome. We talk of cleaner elections and about eliminating the role of black money in them. The role of 'black media', if I may call it so, should receive equal attention if not more.

The other problem with the media, in all its forms, is its excessive preoccupation with the main urban centres, whether it is the national capital, the state capital, or the main towns and cities. It has very little interest in the hinterland and the villages of India. So, however much one sweats it out in the rural areas, the media will show little or no interest in these activities.

Much less effort in the national capital will bring the media swarming all over. This is where the Aam Aadmi Party (AAP) did a smart thing by making Delhi the base of its activities. The national TV channels also double up as regional channels in Delhi. So AAP's day-to-day activities were covered in great detail by the national media and gave it a momentum which it would not have got in any other place or region.

Yet, the people of India have shown from time to time that they can rise above their short-term considerations and right the wrongs in the system. They could defeat, and conclusively, even a powerful prime minister like Indira Gandhi when she made the mistake of imposing Emergency in an attempt to control the lives of the people. Fear was the weapon she used extensively. I cannot forget two scenes, which are etched in my memory.

The JP movement was at its peak in Bihar. JP was to hold a public meeting in Patna's Gandhi Maidan. I was posted in Patna in those days and was returning to the city in a small state government plane after a visit to one of the districts. As we approached Patna, I saw from the air that all the roads, lanes and by-lanes leading to the Gandhi Maidan were choked with people all moving slowly like a glacier towards the Gandhi Maidan. That day's meeting is perhaps the largest meeting ever held in that historic maidan.

Then came the Emergency and, in the same city of Patna, I saw how even small groups of people standing on the road vanished at the sight of a police vehicle. It was fear which drove this behaviour. But this fear vanished when elections were called and the people exercised their franchise in the closet of the polling booth. Do not therefore ever underestimate the fearlessness of the people or their courage when Big Brother is not watching! In booths where the support for the Janata Party was overwhelming, even children queued up to vote. In booth after booth, even the election agents of the mighty Congress Party deserted it.

Three years later, the same Janata Party for which people had voted so overwhelmingly was booted out and Indira Gandhi brought back to power. The one thing people of India find difficult to stomach is the hubris of the democratically elected leaders. The moral of the story for the rulers in India is—let your work speak for you; excessive advertising of your achievements, even if genuine, can ruin your electoral prospects. 'Ye Janata hai ye sub janti hai.'

It is a pity that most of the leaders who emerged from the JP movement lost no time in forgetting the ideals of the movement and became victims of the vices associated with politics. JP had said that his fight was against corruption; yet these leaders established new records in corrupt behaviour. JP was against caste, and during his movement even called upon people to break their sacred threads in public. Yet, his followers emerged as the biggest casteists in Indian politics. JP was against heredity in politics; his followers set up new dynasties in Indian politics. Naturally, JP died a disillusioned and broken man.

Yet, democracy has survived in India despite attacks on its values by its rulers from time to time. Why has it survived in India continuously after Independence, while it has been extinguished elsewhere in the newly independent nations generally, and especially in our neighbourhood, from time to time? It has survived because the people of India are intrinsically tolerant, democratic, secular and liberal in their outlook and character.

Even the hereditary rulers who imbibed these values achieved greatness in our history. Ashoka became great not because he killed his 100 brothers by assassinating them and throwing their bodies in the Agam Kuan of Pataliputra (which still exists), nor by winning the battle of Kalinga, but because he embraced Buddhism, and propagated non-violence and other traditional values of India.

Akbar is considered great not because of his military campaigns but because of the liberal attitude he showed towards the majority of his subjects. Dara Shikoh could not ascend the throne in Delhi, yet he is more respected, even today, than his brother Aurangzeb. As already stated, saints have always been considered superior to the temporal rulers. Bimbisara, the grandfather of Ashoka, abandoned his chariot and walked the rest of the distance to the top of the hill in Rajgir to meet with Buddha. These are some of the eternal values which have held sway throughout history. The values of abnegation and sacrifice are deeply entrenched in our collective character and even if we are unable to practise them ourselves we admire them greatly in others.

It is debatable whether India has achieved all it should have in the seventy years since independence. On the one hand, we have sent the Mangalyaan to explore the planet Mars. Our space agency is capable of launching more than a 100 satellites together. We lead the rest of the world in information technology. Yet, there are hundreds if not thousands of villages which lack the basic amenities of life like an all-weather road, potable drinking water, proper sanitation and health facilities or proper schools. Unemployment continues to be a major problem.

Every government claims to have done its best to solve these problems yet they refuse to go away. Governments are always short on resources; the tax base does not expand despite inspector raj. Only the poor and the innocent are caught and the rich and famous get away. Millions of cases are pending in courts, the jails are full of undertrial prisoners, many of them having spent the maximum jail term which their crime may have merited. There are many ills from which we suffer today. We have miles to go before we rest. But what is the goal that we must set for ourselves for the remaining decades of this century and what are the means by which we can achieve it?

India must strive to reach the top of the league of nations—the top two or three in the world. That is our destiny and we must fulfil it. To arrive there, we must eradicate the bane of poverty, misery and deprivation in our society at the soonest. It is not difficult to achieve this goal.

Our two-pronged strategy should consist of high and sustained economic growth of around 8 per cent per annum for the next twenty years or so and a direct attack on poverty and deprivation. In an uncertain global scenario where globalization is on the retreat and economic nationalism is coming to the fore, we must depend on our own demand, our own resources and our own people to achieve the desired growth rate.

We have massive unmet demand in our economy. Our country is crying out for modern infrastructure. We must build lakhs of kilometres of roads of all kinds, national highways, state highways and rural roads, to connect our country and its people. We need irrigation works especially of the medium and the minor kind to irrigate our still-parched fields. We need all kinds of power, renewable and thermal, to light up our homes, irrigate our fields and run our factories. We need new towns and cities to provide for the population migrating from the rural areas into modern urban centres and to relieve the pressure on farmland and the villages, as well as the existing overcrowded and choking cities. Then, there is the issue of connectivity of these places with modern means of communication like railways and air services, telecom and fast Internet services.

Many more universities are needed and also other centres of excellence. Similarly new research facilities in science and technology are required to meet our growing needs. There is so much to do that the list can go on endlessly. All these activities will contribute to economic growth and generate employment. There will be no dearth of resources. People will always be ready to pay for the services they receive provided they are of quality and are uninterrupted. Resistance comes only when the services supplied are of poor quality and their regular supply is disrupted.

Our Constitution has given primacy to the individual not to the village. I do not know whether that is the reason for the neglect of the village. In the process the individual has also suffered. Is it possible, for a change, to accord primacy to the villages in our country and for the political class to take a vow that the improvement in the quality of the people living in them shall be the first charge on the nation's resources?

A survey should be conducted in all the villages to find out what is lacking there in terms of basic amenities. We should then prepare time-bound plans to provide them with what they need in a pointed, directed manner much in the way in which the doctors treat cancer patients with radiation. In this way, we shall achieve our goal of improving the life of our fellow citizens within the same resources. Liberation of Indian villages from their wants must be our new battle cry.

Underlying all these activities on the nation building front is the need for political and governance reforms. I have already stated above how politics in this country reached its nadir with criminalization and the use of money power in the elections. Some improvement has taken place but a lot remains to be done. A beginning must be made with the democratization of political parties. Internal democracy within most political parties is becoming increasingly rare. Stricter laws, to be enforced by the Election Commission with the threat of de-recognition, are needed to force political parties to abide by these laws and rules.

The patronage available with party bosses for being dispensed to their favourites should be severely curtailed. I am not merely referring to party posts. Nomination to Rajya Sabha and State Legislative Councils is a huge patronage available to even smaller parties and is not subject to any rules within the party. The Left parties do not allow their members the luxury of nomination to these bodies beyond two terms. They strictly adhere to this rule.

The BJP at one time claimed to follow the same rule, but it has been enforced selectively. Leaders who claimed to be wedded to this rule in the case of others have feel no compunction in violating this rule in their own case. Similarly, the rule that people who have lost the Lok Sabha election will not be made ministers has also been violated with impunity. I have nothing against the members of Rajya Sabha, having been one myself on two occasions. But for a politician, it should be considered degrading if he runs away from popular elections and depends only on the patronage of party bosses to continue 'serving' the country through indirect elections.

Considering that conventions have lost their relevance and can be disregarded with impunity, one cannot depend on the good sense of our politicians any more for observing them. We must codify them to the extent possible so that they are preserved in the interest of our democracy.

In governance, the basic principle must be to give more powers to the elected representatives at every level rather than to the permanent bureaucracy. It is ironic that while we trust an elected representative with the key with which nuclear weapons can be unleashed, we are unable to place our trust in elected representatives when it comes to digging a well or constructing a road. Lack of power leads to lack of accountability, which is not good for either democracy or governance.

India's foreign policy has generally been backed by national consensus though there have been occasions where such national consensus has eluded us. We must realize that the sum total of foreign policy is not mere visits to foreign places; it is to understand the limitations of history, the compulsions of geography, the interplay of the national interests of the countries involved and the permanence of those interests.

India lives in a rough neighbourhood. It is our primary national duty to protect the country and its people from external threats and their internal collaborators in this rough neighbourhood. India is the country which has suffered cross-border terrorism for the longest time. This record is a matter of considerable shame for us. No other country of the size and standing of India would have allowed itself this kind of suffering for almost three decades. We cannot depend on the rest of the world to fight our battle for us.

The war against terror is our war; we must fight and win it. While the intruding terrorists must be dealt with by force, the misguided elements within the country that collaborate with them should be dealt with by other means. People turning out in large numbers in Jammu and Kashmir (J&K) in support of terrorists whom our security forces are fighting does not redound to our credit. We are aghast when people in certain areas of J&K shout pro-Pakistan slogans and wave the Pakistani flag, but it exposes our weakness. If my son is guided by my neighbour and does not listen to me it reflects the weakness of his upbringing.

We must seriously reflect why large elements of the population in J&K have turned against us despite all that we claim to have done for them. My own understanding would suggest that we always looked upon J&K as a piece of territory and forgot its people. We forgot that Jammu and Kashmir was the only Muslim majority state which decided to accede to India, not because the Maharajah was a Hindu but because the majority of the people there rejected the two-nation theory of Muhammad Ali Jinnah under the leadership of Sheikh Abdullah. We have failed the people of that state and allowed the issue to remain unresolved for seventy years.

'Will not force is the basis of state,' so said the famous political thinker T.H. Greene. Every democrat believes that consensus, not majoritarianism is the soul of democracy. Liberalism must be the basis of an inclusive state. The mistake we made immediately after we achieved our independence was that, while we embraced liberal democracy for governance, on the economic front, we adopted the restrictive and illiberal socialistic pattern that was another name for the infamous licence-permit-quota raj. Naturally, this deformed combination did not survive and we had to jettison socialism for good in 1991.

Another deformity is raising its head today. This is liberalism on the economic front and sectarianism in politics. And I am not referring to religious fundamentalism alone here. Casteism is equally pernicious. It is an irony that casteists, at times, pretend to be the greatest champions of secularism. Clearly, this is not acceptable. A casteist, by definition, cannot be a secularist.

Rampaging Islamic fundamentalism has emerged as the biggest threat to globalism today. The answer does not lie in a retreat from globalism as some countries are doing. The answer lies in strengthening globalization, in making it more inclusive and equitable.

These are challenging times for India and for the rest of the world. The answers we find today will determine our future for decades to come. Then there will arise new challenges. Journey's end has no end in a nation's march forward.

Rise of the Indian Right to a Hegemonic Role

CHANDAN MITRA

Chandan Mitra has served as a member of Parliament in the Rajya Sabha for two terms, from 2003 to 2016. He is the editor and managing director of the *Pioneer*. He is a well-known journalist with wide-ranging experience in both the print and television media, spanning more than thirty years. An alumnus of La Martiniere Kolkata, St. Stephen's College, Delhi, and Oxford University, he has authored several books, including *Corrupt Society*.

The meteoric rise of the Right in Indian politics and society is a phenomenon that remains to be adequately chronicled. In just about a quarter of a century, a Right-wing party rose from being a virtual pariah to the predominant political force in India, and as of now seems poised to remain at the top of the political and ideological spectrum for the foreseeable future.

This spectacular growth resulted from an amalgam of the rise of religiosity, the global decline of the Left, growing insecurity over the stability of the Hindu civilization perceived to be under threat from cross-border terrorism on the one hand and burgeoning Islamic fundamentalism at home and abroad on the other. Finally, the emergence of a charismatic leadership from within the Bharatiya Janata Party (BJP) and simultaneous erosion of the appeal of leaders of other political faiths helped the BJP to consolidate its support base.

It is not possible to explore all these aspects in detail in one essay. So what will be attempted here is a historical sketch of the rise of the political Right since the early 1990s after being thoroughly badgered at the hands of the Left-liberal ideological forces and the political charisma of Indira Gandhi which nurtured the Left and stymied the Right for decades. It will be also argued that till the almost sudden discovery by the BJP of the mass appeal of the Hindu god-king Ramchandra of Ayodhya around whom the legend of the Ramayana is woven, the Right in India may not have grown at the phenomenal speed that it did, considering its more than modest initial history.

The political Right in India never had a strong ideological or electoral presence almost till the turn of the last century. What went by the definition of Right was basically social conservatism among Hindus, cow protection movements, historically revivalist notions such as recreating Hindu-Pad-Padashahi mooted by Maratha warrior-king Chhatrapati Shivaji and other such romantic, even if obscurantist, ideas.

Before and for decades after Independence, the Right in India was essentially the religious Right, represented by organizations such as the Hindu Mahasabha and the Ram Rajya Parishad. The average success these organizations achieved in north India was in many senses linked to the significant presence of the Arya Samaj, a Hindu social reformist movement led by Swami Dayanand Saraswati. Although anti-idolatry and anti-caste, the Arya Samaj espoused conservative social values. But in the early part of the twentieth century, it found a great deal of traction among the Hindu intelligentsia of Punjab. Most Congress party leaders of Punjab, for instance, were Arya Samajis which drew them into confrontation with the Muslim landed gentry as well as the clergy-led Sikh activists battling to regain control of gurdwaras from Hindu mahants.

Interestingly, recognizing the potential of the Sikh reformists, Mahatma Gandhi threw his weight behind their cause, describing the Jaito Satyagraha of 1921 for 'liberation' of Sikh gurdwaras as the 'first struggle for India's Independence'. While the Jaito Movement led to the consolidation of a Sikh identity and eventually resulted in the rise of the Akali Dal, the ideological evolution of Indian politics was yet to begin. The Partition riots led to a spurt in support for these groups, but not till the RSS became active did the Hindu Right find a significant foothold.

In 1925, Dr Keshav Baliram Hedgewar set up the Rashtriya Swayamsevak Sangh (RSS) in Nagpur, which can be considered the starting point of organized Hindu Right-wing ideology. Subsequently nurtured by ideologues like Veer Savarkar, this was the first serious attempt to define Hindutva as a political, rather than purely religious, idea.

This was an era of competitive communalism as the Muslim League surged spectacularly in the 1930s, especially in UP. When the provincial elections were held in 1936–37 under the Government of India Act of 1935, it gave Indians their first taste of representative government. Thereafter the clash of personalities and ideologies intensified. On the one side was the Left wing, within and outside the Indian National Congress: Organized under the banner of the Congress Socialist Party, it was led by stalwarts like Acharya Narendra Dev, Jayaprakash Narayan, Ram Manohar Lohia, Minoo Masani and some Marxists such as E.M.S. Namboodiripad, who was concurrently a leader of the Communist Party of India (CPI). Within the Congress, there was a prominent Leftist group which included

Jawaharlal Nehru, Subhas Chandra Bose and others. Likewise, there was a Right-wing bloc consisting of leaders like Pandit Madan Mohan Malaviya, who doubled up as prominent members of the Hindu Mahasabha. In other words, both the Left and Right components of the national movement coexisted within the Congress platform. The Right, however, was essentially the religious Right and did not have a separate ideological identity in the sense of espousing a capitalist economic policy.

During World War II, the Leftists broke the association with the Congress, and the CPI went on to lead the anti-Fascist movement which supported the British in the conflict with Germany and Japan. Once Stalin's Soviet Union joined the Allied powers, the Left in India dubbed World War II as a People's War. The ideological Right (that is, those advocating capitalism as the chosen economic policy) remained dormant during the 1930s and 1940s awaiting the conclusion of the war. After Independence, the Congress Socialist Party (CSP) too broke away from the parent party. Paradoxically, some CSP members became founders of India's first non-religious Right-wing political outfit, the Swatantra Party. This was an amalgam of Indian princes and princelings who formed a political outfit called the Ganatantra Parishad. Later they tied up with native industrialists primarily from Bombay, who were bunched together under the Bombay Club, to demand that free India follow classical capitalist economic policies and allow the market to determine the direction of the economy.

Eventually these forces came together to set up the Swatantra Party. Their critique of the Indian government's economic policies was mostly in response to Nehru's progressive shift to the Left, especially after the death of Sardar Vallabhbhai Patel who espoused the cause of a free economy as opposed to Nehru's vision of a controlled economy closely resembling the Soviet model. At the Avadi Session of the All-India Congress Committee (AICC) in 1955, the Congress formally adopted a resolution that proposed a diluted version of that model describing it as the 'socialistic pattern of society' which would pursue a mixed economy model. The party decided by that resolution that the 'commanding heights of the economy' would vest in public hands and the role of the private sector would be subject to government control.

It was in the early 1950s as the country took stock of the ravages of Partition and the devastating Hindu–Muslim riots that happened in its wake that the political Right finally began to take shape. Syama Prasad Mookerjee, a Hindu Mahasabha member of Nehru's first post-Independence cabinet, believed the prime minister to be too soft towards Pakistan. He insisted that Nehru had thus sacrificed the interests of the Hindus of erstwhile East Pakistan and had condemned them to live at the mercy of the Muslim majority in the province. Mookerjee was also incensed by Nehru's deal with then Pakistan Prime Minister Liaquat Ali Khan (the Nehru–Liaquat Pact of 1950) which rejected a transfer of population in the east (unlike Punjab and Sindh). He quit Nehru's cabinet and journeyed to the RSS headquarters in Nagpur. In a meeting with the RSS Sarsanghchalak, M.S. Golwalkar, he advocated the formation of a political party to protect the interests of the Hindus, but one that would stay clear of the obscurantist outfits like the Mahasabha and other such organizations led by Hindu religious leaders, the so-called shankaracharyas, sadhus and sants. Golwalkar agreed to Mookerjee's proposal and it was decided that the RSS would loan two trained organizational hands in each state to the new party named Bharatiya Jana Sangh. Thus in 1952 began the real journey of the organized Right in India under the banner of the Jana Sangh with Mookerjee as its first president and Deen Dayal Upadhyaya, loaned by the RSS, as its general secretary.

More than economic policy, the Indian Right was initially driven by issues of identity and culture, stressing Indianness in every sphere including education. Soon after the Jana Sangh's formation, Mookerjee embarked upon an agitation for the full integration of Jammu and Kashmir with the rest of India, strongly opposing Nehru's decision to grant the erstwhile princely state a special autonomous status under the Constitution through Article 370. To demand abolition of the requirement of Indian citizens to obtain a permit to enter J&K, Mookerjee led a march across the Tawi River bridge and courted arrest in 1952. Chief Minister Sheikh Abdullah's police promptly arrested the Jana Sangh leader who was taken to Srinagar and interned in an isolated guest house despite his failing health. Not surprisingly, Mookerjee died shortly thereafter, allegedly due to insufficient medical care, causing widespread revulsion in the rest of India against Nehru's kid-glove treatment of Sheikh Abdullah. The Jana Sangh's slogan: '*Ek desh mein do pradhan, do vidhan, do nishan nehi chalenge* [One country cannot have two prime ministers, two Constitutions and two flags]', gained wide currency in the aftermath of Mookerjee's untimely death.

Under Article 370, Jammu and Kashmir was permitted to have a separate Constitution and its own flag which was to be flown on government buildings concurrently with the national tricolour. The state's chief minister was officially designated as Wazir-e-Azam (equivalent to prime minister). Although the import of these provisions has been considerably diluted, starting with Sheikh Abdullah's arrest in 1953, they remain a sore point with India's Right.

The demand for the abolition of Kashmir's special status remains a cornerstone of India's Right wing to this date, and the BJP continues to oppose the existence of Article 370 in the statute books although successive BJP-led governments in Delhi have not yet taken meaningful steps to abolish the provision.

Apart from the full unification of Kashmir with the rest of India, the other major issue championed by the Right was cow protection. Ban on cow slaughter was enshrined in the Directive Principles of the Constitution, in keeping with the pre-Independence demand of the Congress. It was always an article of faith with Mahatma Gandhi who wrote extensively on the subject. But this was a communally divisive issue and had resulted in frequent riots between Hindus and Muslims. After Independence, the issue failed to gain much traction in the initial years till the Bharat Sadhu Samaj, an association of Hindu priests, launched an agitation in the mid-1960s. This culminated in a huge demonstration by saffron-robed priests and other men of religion outside the Parliament House in 1967, resulting in police firing and the death of several protestors. The then home minister, Gulzarilal Nanda, who had a soft spot for the Sadhu Samaj, resigned from the cabinet in the wake of the police action but was reinducted after some time.

Although successive governments refused to enact a law banning the slaughter of cows across India, the demand kept surfacing from time to time. The Jana Sangh continued to agitate for its implementation but never got sufficient electoral support. The issue was left to the states and it is only under the present Narendra Modi government that several state governments commenced implementation of the ban over the last three years.

India's economic policy was guided by Nehruvian socialist ideas, and the domination of the public sector was supreme. India's was also a closed economy, with severe curbs on imports of foreign consumer goods and limited access to foreign exchange. Industrialization remained stunted as official sanction was required to start industries. The 'licence-permit raj' dominated domestic economic policy from the 1950s to the early 1990s, and it confined India to what was derisively called the 'Hindu rate of growth', averaging approximately 3.5 per cent per annum.

Economic policy took a sharp Left turn in the late 1960s soon after Indira Gandhi assumed office as prime minister in 1966. India faced a severe drought that year and the next, particularly affecting Bihar. New Delhi had to run to Washington with a begging bowl for wheat from the US. The Americans forced a dilution of Indira Gandhi's pro-Soviet foreign policy, over Vietnam in particular, before agreeing to supply grain to India under the Public Loan (PL) 480 scheme. Food stocks hit rock bottom and ration shops were left with virtually no supplies.

Economic wags commented that India was forced to eke out a 'ship to mouth existence', waiting for wheat-laden American vessels to dock in Bombay so that supplies could be transported to ration shops across India.

Even as food riots broke out in many parts of the country, especially West Bengal, Indira Gandhi played a political master stroke by shifting attention to her critics in the Congress Party, blaming the party's Old Guard for the country's economic ills. Instead of recognizing that her father's policy to ensure a 'socialistic pattern of society' and overemphasis on industry to the detriment of agriculture were responsible for the economic mess, she blamed the Right wing of the party led by Finance Minister Morarji Desai and Bombay strongman S.K. Patil for the nation's woes. Just when experts argued for liberalization, she tightened controls starting with a dramatic announcement nationalizing major private banks. Simultaneously she abolished privy purses enjoyed by erstwhile feudal rulers of many principalities. In other words, the Right wing was demonized further and the virtues of the Left and socialism extolled.

The Right, a relatively marginal political force, was pushed even deeper into a corner. The Jana Sangh, along with the Swatantra Party that led the Right in the 1967 parliamentary elections—which saw the Congress reduced to a minority for the first time since Independence—was on the ascendancy since 1967 when the party stalwarts led several non-Congress alliance governments in many north Indian states. However, by sharply turning Left with a slew of populist measures, Indira Gandhi successfully combated the Right both within and outside the Congress Party.

In Indira Gandhi's socialist heyday, the Indian Right was marginalized yet again. The Swatantra Party virtually came apart. The princelings became objects of ridicule after Indira Gandhi boldly abolished their privileges and scrapped their 'royal' titles. The Jana Sangh was the only Right-wing political outfit to survive Gandhi's Leftist onslaught, mainly due to the cadre-based support of the RSS. Her popularity increased after the Left turn and 'pink' economic policies. Soviet support for her grew steadily and Indian communists (CPI in particular) were directed to support her domestically. (Since the party's division in 1964 and formation of the more radical CPI-M, communists were often in a quandary but broadly supported her socialist policies.)

The Indian Right, or whatever was left of it, was laid low by Indira Gandhi's aggressive policies. She was further helped by the Bangladesh Liberation War in which the then US President, Richard Nixon, famously 'tilted' towards Pakistan and even dispatched a US aircraft carrier into the Bay of Bengal. But for all the accolades she won and despite a huge electoral triumph in 1971, the economic situation at home worsened due to her stubborn socialist policies. However, at that time, Indira Gandhi was like a goddess who could do no wrong and her Right-wing critics in the Jana Sangh were a discredited lot. But as the economic situation worsened, the Right got an opportunity to expand, starting in Bombay where local textile workers were losing jobs due to a recession and white-collar jobs were increasingly being grabbed by non-Maharashtrians. Giving vent to their angst, Balasaheb Thackeray, a cartoonist by profession, founded the Shiv Sena to fight the communists that dominated the trade unions and south Indian migrants who increasingly pushed out the natives from clerical jobs.

The Shiv Sena, using a potent mix of aggressive 'sons of the soil' ideology and considerable muscle power, successfully ousted the communists—both blue- and white-collar—from control of trade unions. The organization routinely used strong-arm methods to coerce non-Maharashtrians into either leaving Bombay or extravagantly funding the Sena as protection money. Sena's politics was of identity alone and it did not have any deep religious background beyond organizing lavish Ganpati pujas that were popular in any case. Thus the Shiv Sena was perhaps the first fightback by the Right against the Left/socialist policies of the dominant parties. After vanquishing the unions, the Sena turned to full-fledged politics, and Bal Thackeray's extraordinary popularity enabled it to establish a base all over Bombay and subsequently other regions of Maharashtra, notably the Konkan coast.

On the national scale, however, the Right received a further drubbing in the mid-1970s when Indira Gandhi, with son Sanjay in tow, launched a full-scale offensive against the so-called fascist forces. This term was a euphemism for the entire non-Left Opposition, such as the Congress(O) and Jana Sangh which trounced her party, then known as Congress(R) following a split in 1969, in the Gujarat state assembly polls in 1974. This roughly coincided with a national railway strike organized by firebrand trade unionist George Fernandes. The strike brought the economy virtually to its knees. Not even the nuclear 'implosion' in Pokhran that year helped stem the tide of opposition to Indira Gandhi and her 'socialist' policies.

Ironically, she had won a spectacular victory in the 1971 general election and followed it up with the vivisection of Pakistan in December 1971, whereby Bangladesh was created and it briefly took her popularity to dizzy heights. An outwitted Opposition succumbed to her charisma with even the Jana Sangh leader and acclaimed parliamentarian Atal Bihari Vajpayee comparing her to Goddess Durga in the aftermath of India's victory over Pakistan in the 1971 war.

However, alarmed by the sudden erosion of her popularity barely two years down the line, Gandhi resumed her combative politics against the Opposition, targeting the so-called Right wing, particularly the RSS. The non-Left Opposition, meanwhile, persuaded respected Gandhian socialist Jayaprakash Narayan to become its mascot. Although an associate of Jawaharlal Nehru, he was subjected to a vicious attack by Nehru's grandson Sanjay Gandhi. Sanjay and his supporters clubbed together under a rejuvenated Youth Congress whose intimidatory tactics were akin to German storm troopers of the Nazi era.

Following a judicial verdict which unseated Gandhi from the Rae Bareli Lok Sabha seat for 'corrupt electoral practices', she decided to abandon all pretence to democratic commitment. Invoking a little-known constitutional provision, which allowed the government to declare an internal Emergency, Gandhi, on 26 June 1975, arrested all senior non-Left opposition leaders, imposed censorship on the media, which had largely turned hostile to her and her son, and implemented draconian measures including suspension of fundamental rights and independence of the judiciary. All along Gandhi's Leftist rhetoric grew shriller and her party continued to badger the Right for posing largely imaginary threats to her government.

Paradoxically, however, the Emergency enabled the Right wing, especially the RSS to spread its tentacles. When all overground opposition leaders were put behind bars, the RSS's lesser-known activists had a field day, spreading disaffection against the authoritarian Indira regime mainly through rumours disseminated at milk booths, bus stops and train compartments. Stories of police excesses reached far and wide, often with gross exaggeration and the mother–son duo of the Congress was massively demonized. Sanjay Gandhi's determination to curb population growth added a new dimension to the subterranean protests.

Muslims, hitherto loyal supporters of the Congress Party and Gandhi personally, resented the imposition of population control measures, whereby able-bodied men were picked up at random and vasectomy conducted on them. Government servants including schoolteachers were tasked to bring such persons to makeshift medical camps housed in tents, even in remote villages. They were given individual and collective targets by the district administration. 'Nasbandi' or vasectomy spread terror across the countryside, especially in north India, and thousands of villages were bereft of males of reproductive age, who fled to nearby jungles or other places where they could not be easily located.

When the Emergency was relaxed in January 1977 to allow the holding of the general election (already delayed by one year through an executive order), the pent-up anger of the people erupted in unexpected fury. Relaxation of censorship allowed newspapers (particularly non-Congress supporting publications such as the *Indian Express* and the *Statesman*) to publish hundreds of reports that had been 'killed' by the censor. This led to an outpouring of revulsion against the Emergency regime. Many opposition leaders released from jail began planning to take on Gandhi and their efforts bore fruit when the Congress(O), Jana Sangh, Charan Singh's Bharatiya Kranti Dal (BKD) and various socialists merged under the moral guidance of Jayaprakash Narayan to form the Janata Party. To the nation's as well as Indira Gandhi's own shock and awe, the Congress was routed in the March 1977 polls.

Unbelievably, both Gandhi and Sanjay Gandhi lost their own seats as did most Congress stalwarts. Although the opposition parties had officially merged and Chandra Shekhar was named party president, there was no meeting of minds. The Jana Sangh component emerged as the largest within the Janata Party ensemble. Possibly, at the instigation of some Congress and Left leaders, Raj Narain, an eccentric socialist and health minister in the Morarji Desai-led Janata Party government mounted a fierce campaign against the Jana Sangh on the grounds that all members of the party were guilty of dual loyalty by virtue of their simultaneous allegiance to the RSS.

Barely had it recovered from Indira Gandhi's sustained onslaught before and during the Emergency when the Indian Right suffered yet another blow. They had hardly begun the process of consolidating their ideological gains in government positions when the first Union government with a Right-wing party in a prominent position lost power, thanks to the combined machinations of the maverick socialist Raj Narain and Congress's power-hungry strategist Sanjay Gandhi. After thirty months of political instability, Indira Gandhi was back in power with a thumping majority in the 1980 midterm elections. The Right was again out on a limb and Gandhi not only systematically ousted Jana Sangh/Swatantra Party nominees from positions of authority but also dismissed state governments of the Janata Party.

The Indian Right had lost whatever gains it had made in the period between 1974 and 1979 and even the Jana Sangh was back to square one. In this period, Indira Gandhi weaned herself away from the Left, an ideology detested by Sanjay Gandhi who had mounted an offensive on the party's ally, the CPI, at the Guwahati session of the AICC, made infamous by party president Dev Kanta Borooah's comment, 'India is Indira.' Having played footsie with the Left for long, Indira Gandhi initiated the process of isolating the Left everywhere, forgetting that it was the Left's support that enabled her to lead a minority government after the Congress split. It was their support that also ensured victory for her candidate, V.V. Giri, as President of India against the official Congress nominee, N. Sanjiva Reddy. But confident of full authority after her 1980 victory, Indira Gandhi started wooing the Right, especially Hindu religious forces, visiting temples and performing pujas.

To an extent her new-found tilt towards religiosity was driven by the rise of Sikh fundamentalism in Punjab under the burgeoning malevolent halo of a preacher-turned-separatist, Jarnail Singh Bhindranwale. In hindsight it is clear that it was Gandhi who initially encouraged the rise of Bhindranwale in an effort to curtail the influence of the Akali Dal. In order to counter rising Sikh fundamentalism, Gandhi took a soft

Hindutva position, a far cry from her past ideological and political upbringing.

The old adage 'If you sow the wind, be prepared to reap the whirlwind' turned out to be tragically true in her case, when in an act of revenge against the Indian army's assault on the Golden Temple in Amritsar in June 1984, which resulted in an estimated 700 deaths including that of Bhindranwale, India's prime minister was shot dead by two of her own bodyguards within the compound of her official residence—1, Safdarjung Road. The murder resulted in an outburst of violent frenzy and massacre of Sikhs mainly in Delhi, under the instigation of various local Congress party leaders.

Gandhi's younger son Sanjay who was being groomed as her successor had died in a plane crash in 1980, leading to his elder brother Rajiv being anointed prime minister on the very day of her murder. Rajiv Gandhi quickly called a general election to ratify his succession and stunned the Opposition by winning 410 seats out of 543 in the Lok Sabha, the Congress Party's best ever performance. Rajiv Gandhi carried no ideological baggage and if anything was a Right-of-Centre leader who believed in India's rapid computerization. He was also not enamoured of the public sector, and the spate of nationalization that happened during Gandhi's tenure came to an abrupt stop. But politically, the Congress was still seen as Left-of-Centre, carrying forward Gandhi's programme of 'Garibi Hatao'. Given the ruling party's brute majority in Parliament (which prompted Atal Bihari Vajpayee to describe it as Shok Sabha—assembly of mourners—rather than Lok Sabha), neither the Left nor Right was in a position to assert for some years. In fact, the Bharatiya Janata

Party, new avatar of the Bharatiya Jana Sangh, was reduced to a cipher, winning just two seats in Parliament in the 1984 general election.

The Right got its next break when Rajiv Gandhi lost popularity on account of a scandal involving the purchase of 155 mm howitzers for the Indian army from Sweden's AB Bofors—a major international arms manufacturer. One of his more upright ministers, V.P. Singh, quit to form his own Jan Morcha Party which joined hands with other opposition groups and secured outside support from both the Right and the Left.

V.P. Singh led the newly formed Janata Dal to a historic victory in 1989, and the Right again saw a flicker of hope as the Congress was ousted from power. But a cagey V.P. Singh, insecure at the thought that the Haryana strongman Devi Lal would upstage him through a massive public rally, announced the immediate implementation of the Mandal Commission's Report, recommending 27 per cent reservation for the so-called Other Backward Classes in government jobs and access to government-run educational institutions. Massive countrywide protests followed. Some students attempted self-immolation at public places to arouse public anger. Discomfited by this socially divisive development, both the Congress and BJP wanted an early ouster of the V.P. Singh government. Chandra Shekhar became the prime minister with Congress's support, but his government lasted merely four months as Congress pulled the rug and pushed for another early election.

That is when the Right got its first electoral break. By 1989, when the midterm election was called, two significant developments had happened. First, the BJP adopted a resolution at its national council meeting in Palampur, Himachal Pradesh, lending full support to the Vishwa Hindu Parishad's long-standing demand for the building of a Ram temple at Bhagwan Ram's birthplace in Ayodhya. Second, the VHP launched a countrywide movement to collect 'Ram shila' or bricks consecrated in the name of Ram which were brought to Ayodhya by various means of transport including bullock carts. The journey of trucks, vans and carts across villages and cities of India created a near-hysteria with thousands of people, especially women lining the route, showering the bricks with Ganga water, flowers and monetary donations to help the construction of the Ram temple.

It was the focus on building a Ram Mandir where the Babri Masjid stood that truly propelled the Indian Right led by the BJP to a dominant political position. A brainchild of the then BJP president Lal Krishna Advani, the adoption of the Ram Mandir agenda enabled the party to spread its wings all over the country. Advani's other coinage, pseudo-secularism, a term used to describe the apparent hypocrisy—politics of appeasement to be precise—of the Congress and its Left fellow travellers helped further augment its intellectual argument against the double standards of the mainstream 'secular' parties which the BJP accused of minority appeasement. These groups never imagined that invocation of Bhagwan Ram, a proto-historic god-king of Ayodhya, would arouse such political passion. They continued to rubbish Ram and myths associated with him. The more they ridiculed Ram, the more the BJP's support on this score grew.

Emergence of Ram as a Political Icon

Bol Siyavar Ramchandra ki jai!
Pawansut Hanuman ki jai!
Swatantra Bharat ki jai!

Jayaprakash Narayan, Gandhian socialist leader and architect of Indira Gandhi's ignominious defeat in the 1977 elections, cites this chant as an instance of the idea of freedom gripping the Indian imagination in the mid-1930s. In his memoirs, JP, as he was popularly known, recalls travelling through remote villages in Bihar campaigning for the Congress during the provincial elections of 1936. One chilly autumn night, as his bullock cart passed by a Ramlila venue, JP remembers waking up from his slumber upon hearing this cry. He writes he was astonished to find a nationalist slogan effortlessly blending with a centuries-old religious exhortation. That, he said, made him realize that Independence was an idea whose time had come. When a contemporary political goal gets fused with deep-rooted religious/cultural faith, wrote JP, it signifies the moral validity of the political ideal, in this case the struggle for freedom from the British rule.

Cut to 1989–92: First Uttar Pradesh and then almost the whole of north India reverberated to the slogans—'*Ram Lalla hum aaye hain/ Mandir yahin banayenge* and *Saugandh Ram ki khaate hain/ Mandir wahin banayenge* [O Child Ram, we have come to build your temple on this very spot and We swear by Ram, the temple will be built right there]'. Following a succession of massive congregations organized by the Vishwa

Hindu Parishad and supported by the Bharatiya Janata Party, at the spot where the Babri Masjid stood, on 6 December 1992 thousands of kar sewaks (voluntary workers) demolished the huge, 400-year-old, triple-domed mosque built by Mir Baqi, a general in India's first Mughal king's, Babur's, army. The structure was pulled down by thousands of assembled Hindu activists virtually with bare hands.

The denouement heralded a cataclysmic change in contemporary Indian politics and forever altered the national discourse. It also catapulted the Bharatiya Janata Party to the status of an alternate pole in Indian politics, destroying the Congress's monopoly of power since Independence and presaged untold consequences for the country.

How did Ramchandra, god-king of Ayodhya, a small principality 120 kilometres north-east of the present Uttar Pradesh capital of Lucknow, come to acquire such supreme political significance? Although the Ramayana is among the world's favourite legends, told and retold over millennia across the entire sphere of Hindu cultural influence including South East Asia, it was never regarded as a political legend. In fact, that status more appropriately fits the other great Hindu epic, Mahabharata, with its tales of intrigue, conspiracy and struggle for power between the Kauravas and Pandavas. The Mahabharata is replete with political lessons that hold true several thousand years after the original was penned, centred around an eighteen-day historical war between the two warring branches of the Bharata clan fought on the plains of Kurukshetra, venue for many subsequent wars for the control of north India.

The Ramayana, on the other hand, is a relatively soft story that dwells more on everyday human emotions. Its main protagonist embodies the laudable values of truthfulness, filial devotion, love, kindness, affection, retribution against the lustful, valour in battle, commitment to fair play, supremacy of justice and duties of a monarch towards his subjects. Most north Indians revere Raja Ramchandra as Maryada Purushottam—greatest of men, upholder of morality—and it is rare for a learned person to refer to him without this prefix.

The principal factor behind the 'politicization' of Ram over the years was the reality that a Muslim general constructed a mosque at the most visible spot in the preponderantly Hindu town of Ayodhya soon after Babur conquered Delhi in 1526. The Babri Masjid stood on a hillock overlooking the town, clearly the obvious site for an ancient palace. Without going into the historical or archaeological debate about whether Mir Baqi demolished the ruins of the palace where Ram was supposedly born and erected a mosque in its place to declare Muslim supremacy over Hindustan, it can be safely asserted that most Hindus have always believed that to be true. Efforts to recapture the mosque began barely 100 years after it was built, and ragtag Hindu armies led by various holy men repeatedly mounted assaults on the structure. Historical accounts detail the enormous casualties resulting from the frequent armed clashes between Hindu groups and Muslim defenders of the shrine.

Exasperated with these disputes and fearing more breaches of law and order, the British administration banned the collective offering of namaz in 1939, but allowed individual members of both communities to enter the outer precincts of the shrine to worship in accordance with their respective beliefs. The Babri Masjid stood amid gathering storm clouds as Hindus increasingly flexed their muscle in the wake of the freedom struggle. But the neighbouring Muslim-dominated city of Faizabad, once the capital of the nawabs of Oudh, routinely dispatched volunteers to guard the masjid from physical harm.

Following Independence, the movement to 'liberate' the Ram Mandir gathered fresh momentum. In 1949, under the benign gaze of a Keralite district magistrate, K.K. Nair, idols of the infant Ram were allegedly smuggled into the complex and quietly installed. Hindus concluded this to be a miracle whereby Ram had reasserted the right to his original home. That led to great jubilation with Hindus thronging the shrine in thousands to worship the image and celebrate the 'liberation' of the shrine. Nair, after retiring from the Indian Civil Service, formally joined politics and was even elected member of Parliament as a nominee of the Hindu Mahasabha in the first general election of 1952.

The agnostic Prime Minister Jawaharlal Nehru, who had no patience for religious exhibitionism, repeatedly exhorted his Congress colleagues in Uttar Pradesh to nip Hindu assertiveness in the bud. But successive chief ministers, Govind Ballabh Pant and Sampurnanand, fearful of a backlash, politely ignored Nehru's exhortations.

From 1949 to 1986, the Babri Masjid stood in forlorn isolation. Under court orders Hindu priests were allowed to enter its locked precincts twice a day to offer prayers that were witnessed from behind colossal iron bars by a small crowd of locals and occasional pilgrims from other parts of India.

Meanwhile the British court order restraining Muslims from coming within 200 yards of the mosque remained in force. On Fridays, a handful of devotees assembled at a distance and offered namaz, much to the chagrin of Hindus. Altercations and fisticuffs took place regularly, but the presence of a strong police force at the spot prevented the eruption of large-scale intercommunity violence for nearly forty years. The issue lay dormant for years, although Hindus routinely thronged the shrine on festive occasions such as Ram Navami, but had to be content with darshan from outside the iron bars of the locked gate. Only a few priests were permitted inside under police escort under court orders, enabling them to offer ritual prayers. But no mainstream political party raised the issue in a significant way and both Hindus and Muslims seemed reconciled to judicial orders freezing the dispute pending settlement of conflicting claims to the land on which the shrine stood. The Hindu Mahasabha, which was the only political outfit to have listed its 'liberation' in its manifestos, declined as an electoral force in the 1960s with the less orthodox Bharatiya Jana Sangh, precursor of the BJP, gradually appropriating the 'Hindu' political space with the powerful backing of the RSS. Neither the Jana Sangh nor the BJP made Ram Mandir an electoral plank till much later.

That the issue had not entirely vanished from the public domain became apparent when, in a surprise move, Rajiv Gandhi's government suddenly withdrew the prosecution case in April 1986, allowing the shrine to be unlocked and giving unrestricted access to Hindus to worship the idol of Ram Lalla neatly placed under the central dome of the mosque. The baffling move was intended as an attempt to mollify Hindus who were angry over the government's decision to enact a law that overturned a court order permitting alimony to divorced Muslim women. This too-clever-by-half ploy was a transparent effort to pacify orthodox Muslims and then balance it by courting agitated Hindu groups. But the reopening of the shrine's gate had an electrifying effect and multitudes from across the country descended on Ayodhya to have a close darshan of the idol. Meanwhile, the RSS front organization Vishwa Hindu Parishad launched a movement for the construction of an appropriate mandir on the spot, mobilizing people through a nationwide 'shila pujan'. This entailed collection of bricks from devotees, which were then consecrated, called 'Ram shila', and carried in processions throughout the country. The bricks were brought to Ayodhya for 'shila pujan', which, surprisingly again, was permitted by the government on the 'undisputed' land just outside the structure in November 1989. Seizing the initiative in response to growing Hindu assertiveness, the BJP, at its national council meeting in Palampur in Himachal Pradesh that year, formally incorporated the VHP's demand in its political agenda. Ram's emergence as a political icon, the rallying point for a robust nationalist ideal, owes itself primarily to the Somnath–Ayodhya Rath Yatra undertaken by BJP leader Lal Krishna Advani in 1990. Although widely criticized by sections of the media and political class for being obscurantist, revanchist, majoritarian and socially divisive, the Rath Yatra evoked a public response hitherto not experienced in independent India. Critics said it was the 'Hindu revivalist' BJP's crude attempt to counter the impact of job reservations for backward castes promulgated by the V.P. Singh government, which Hindu leaders believed was a recipe for social disintegration. Advani could not reach Ayodhya in his motorized chariot as he was arrested by then Bihar Chief Minister Lalu Prasad Yadav, a staunch opponent of the BJP's philosophy. But the near-hysteria generated across the country by this novel method of mass mobilization, served the BJP's political purpose well. It also catapulted Ram to the status of central deity in the Hindu pantheon besides establishing him as a powerful symbol of cross-caste Hindu unity. Till then, no religious figure, be it Ram, Krishna or even Shiva, had ever been used for political mobilization on a significant scale although Mahatma Gandhi's message to the masses was replete with Hindu imagery, particularly the concept of Ram Rajya—restoration of the golden age of justice and social harmony symbolized by Ramchandra's rule in Ayodhya. The emergence of Ram as a powerful instrument of political mobilization was undoubtedly facilitated by the television serial *Ramayana*, which preceded the resurrection of the Ayodhya movement. The televised version of the epic brought it alive to a new generation of Indians who were no longer sufficiently exposed to this riveting tale, which was usually narrated to children by grandmothers at home in earlier times and dramatized through Ramlila performances before the Dussehra festival every year.

In retrospect, it can be asserted that the revival of Ram's appeal via the telecast had a lot to do with reinforcing his iconic stature. It was Advani's perceptive ability to grasp the developing public mood that enabled him to catalyse the impact of the serial into a political instrument. In the process, Ram progressively acquired the position of a political cult.

In a sense, the emergence of Ram as a political icon has a lot to do with the Hindu psyche that abhors militarism and usually reacts politically only under grave provocation, real or perceived. Unlike, say, Arjun, hero of Mahabharat, Ram is seen to be flawless as an individual and also the embodiment of *rajdharma* (duties of a ruler). In the late 1980s and early 1990s, Indian society was undergoing an unprecedented churning. Many comfortable certainties of the Nehru–Indira years had suddenly disappeared. The upper castes, in particular, were gravely discomfited by the rise of crass vote-bank politics whereby politicians sought to carve caste-based niches to jump the queue and grab power. In the legendary persona of Ram, this section of the Hindus sought an assurance of stability, continuity and reaffirmation of traditional values. Analysts believe Hindu angst got spent with the uncalled-for demolition of the Babri Masjid. In fact, the community was probably gripped by a sense of remorse that a shrine had been desecrated thus. When the Narasimha Rao regime (1991–96) dismissed four BJP-run state governments in the wake of the demolition, the party lost all those states in the midterm polls held just six months after the event, barely clinging on to power only in Rajasthan with the help of defectors. Since its 1993 defeat in Uttar Pradesh where Ayodhya is located, the BJP has been in steady decline as an electoral force in that state.

So, was Ram's emergence as a political icon ephemeral? The jury is still out on this. Although the VHP has sought to periodically revive the agitation to regain the land, cordoned off under court orders and housing only a makeshift, tented temple in which the idols are worshipped under frightening security cover, its efforts have largely met with indifference. The BJP, after its six-year stint in power at the Centre, now seeks to project itself more as a modern Right-of-Centre party on the lines of Europe's Christian Democrats. Although the cry of 'Jai Shri Ram' is still heard at BJP rallies, it carries lesser and lesser conviction. The ultra-Right, in fact, accuses the BJP of using Ram to position itself as the principal political alternative to the Congress and thereafter jettisoning the king of Ayodhya. Ram Lalla, for whom millions fought pitched battles over four centuries, meanwhile languishes, forlorn inside a tattered tent. Ram may still retain politically iconic stature, but, ironically, his idol remains in what resembles a refugee camp rather than the magnificent temple he was promised.

The assessment that Hindu anger was spent with the demolition of the Babri Masjid was based not only on the religious Right's failure to resume a feisty campaign for a grand temple's construction in Ayodhya, but also because the VHP's war cry for the 'liberation' of two other Hindu holy shrines in Varanasi and Mathura, desecrated by Mughal Emperor Aurangzeb, did not gather steam. But after a spell of somnolence, the Hindu Right began to organize itself more systematically, although the thrust for its resurgence was mainly political rather than religious.

The Right scored a major triumph when the BJP, under the leadership of the relatively benign Atal Bihari Vajpayee, organizationally steered by strongman Lal Krishna Advani came to power in alliance with a multitude of regional parties in 1996. But the National Democratic Alliance had a wafer-thin majority and Vajpayee's second government (the first lasted exactly thirteen days) too was felled by one vote in a no confidence motion in the Parliament in 1998.

The NDA returned to power with a clear majority in 1999 and its government furthered the Right-wing economic thrust initiated by Congress Prime Minister Narasimha Rao under pressure from the International Monetary Fund. Economic liberalization was the buzzword at this time and Indira Gandhi's socialist policies were abandoned altogether. This was a shared understanding between the Congress and BJP and consequently the rise of Right-wing economics was complete. Despite running a government successfully for five straight years, Vajpayee faced a shock defeat in 2004. The Congress, although no longer Left-oriented, returned to power and the mild-mannered Manmohan Singh led a reformist Right-oriented government till 2014, trouncing the BJP's challenge under Advani's leadership once again in 2009. But the political Right would no longer be so easily overcome. It had grown deep ideological roots and the Congress's lacklustre leadership since the assassination of Rajiv Gandhi in 1991 was unable to hold on to the reins of power for long.

The Right in India is a formidable force today. Politically, the BJP is ruling at the Centre with a huge majority in the Lok Sabha and by 2018 will have a majority in the Upper House too. It is in power singly or in alliance with junior partners in fourteen states. More than two-thirds of India's population of 125 crore live in BJP-ruled states. In March 2017, the party won a stunning victory in Uttar Pradesh, the country's largest state. The head of a religious institution, the Gorakhnath Math of Gorakhpur, saffron-robed Yogi Adityanath was named chief minister of the state while in neighbouring Uttarakhand an RSS preacher, Trivendra Singh Rawat, has assumed charge as head of the state government. Prime Minister Modi's popularity remains unchallenged.

It can be safely asserted that no leader has reached such dizzy heights of popular acclaim since Indira Gandhi. The BJP, backed by the RSS cadre, has made inroads into think tanks, academic institutions and other instruments of statecraft. Ideologically, the Left has been decimated for all practical purposes unless Maoist insurgents are included in Left ranks. The CPI(M) hangs on to power only in Tripura and Kerala, while the only major state still in the Congress's control is Karnataka. At this point of time, the political Right represented by the BJP appears unassailable.

It has been a long and tortuous journey for the Right, defeating Leftist and quasi-Leftist forces over the last sixty years. With the BJP replacing the Congress as the biggest national party with 10 crore members, the Right has good reason to celebrate its success.

Addressing Nellie

DEREK O'BRIEN

Derek O'Brien is a politician, author, television personality and public speaker. He is a two-time member of the Rajya Sabha from West Bengal, representing the Trinamool Congress. His speeches and writings on issues of national importance are discussed widely in national and international media. He has spoken at leading educational institutions around the world. In 2012, he addressed the United Nations General Assembly.

Each year, on 15 August, I find myself thinking of my great-grandmother—my father's paternal grandmother. Nellie Bella Biswas, as she was named when born to a Bengali-Christian family with homes in Jalpaiguri in north Bengal and Maniktala in north Kolkata, formed part of my earliest memories. She died in 1969, when I was just a schoolboy. Even by then she had come to represent an influential figure for me—the familiar matriarch, caring but firm, who taught the three of us, my brothers and me, to speak Bengali.

To my young mind, Nellie Bella Biswas—or Nellie Bella O'Brien as she became on marrying the descendant of an Irish settler in India—symbolized history. She was a walking, talking monument of history. To my innocent eyes, she seemed to stand for Mother India: a venerable and iconic figure who shed a silent tear in August 1947 as one country became two nations, and a composite society was split forever.

Nellie cried in August 1947, she cried every day from 1947 to 1969. She cried for the line in the sand that Partition drew.

She cried for Patrick, her firstborn, her beloved son, who stayed on in Lahore . . .

For obvious reasons, the narrative of Partition has been written in terms of the subcontinent's Hindus and Muslims. Christians have had only a small role in this drama. Anglo-Indians—the community I belong to and which makes up a minuscule section of India's Christians—have not even had a walk-on part.

Yet Partition had a dramatic impact on my extended family. My paternal grandfather, Amos, was one of the three brothers. The eldest of them, Patrick, was a civil servant who worked in Lahore and Peshawar, and served as a private secretary to Sir Olaf Caroe and later Sir George Cunningham, governors of the North-West Frontier Province in the tumultuous days leading up to August 1947. Much of the rest of the family, including my father and grandfather, were in Kolkata (or Calcutta, as it was then called).

One day, without quite realizing the implications, these members of the O'Brien family became citizens of separate countries. Patrick, the brother who had stayed on in Pakistan, had a large family. Two of his daughters were married to fighter pilots of what was at the time the Royal Indian Air Force. In 1947, they were either allotted or chose different nations.

Within months India and Pakistan were at war. It was a conflict that tore apart my father's cousins, daughters of Patrick. One of them was with her father in Pakistan. Her husband was a fighter pilot in the Pakistan Air Force, her sister's husband a fighter pilot in the Indian Air Force.

Night after night she stayed up, wondering if her husband would come home or if her brother-in-law in India was safe, or if these two men so dear to her, comrades and friends in the same air force till only a few weeks earlier, would aim for each other in the eerie anonymity of the skies. Her sister in India went through the same trauma. Patrick comforted his daughter. In another country, Nellie comforted her granddaughter.

Thankfully, neither man died in that war, but a distance emerged. Father and daughter, sister and sister, cousin and cousin, my Indian grandfather and his Pakistani brother—they lost touch with each other.

* * *

Today, those times seem so far away. My brothers and I grew up in a very different environment in the 1960s and 1970s. We were not just a minority, we often joked, but a minority in a minority in a minority: Roman Catholics among Anglo-Indians among Indian Christians. Javed Khan, a friend and colleague in the Trinamool Congress, once told me in a lighter moment that Muslims were the 'majority minority' and we Christians the 'minority minority'.

Beyond those laughs, what does it mean to be a minority in India? Frankly, I don't think I can give a complete answer, and I doubt anyone can. I will try and explain it, though, from three angles—that of my family and me; my community; and the larger social contract between religious minorities and the nation we have built. These are reflections based on my experiences. They may or may not speak for everybody, but I hope they will explain, in some measure, the miracle of an India that allows an Anglo-Indian to enter the Parliament as a representative of a largely Bengali party.

I grew up in the only Christian family in a middle-class, predominantly Bengali-Hindu neighbourhood in Kolkata, living in, one of those ironies that make India just so captivating, a lane named after a Muslim. There were three of us, three boys. From the beginning, there was a pressure to fit in, not from the people next door but from our own parents and Nellie. We were pushed to learn the local language.

Not everybody in the Anglo-Indian community saw things as my parents did. Many insisted on speaking in English and in a pidgin, caricatural Hindi. Some decided that India was not for them and migrated. The numbers in our churches and community gatherings declined. The railways, the post and the telegraph departments, the Indian school system—all those great institutions that had been Anglo-Indian bastions began to acquire a different flavour. The mood was downbeat.

It began to change in the mid-1990s, as the Indian economy started to grow, throwing up new opportunities, particularly in the services sector. Suddenly the very qualities that had made Anglo-Indians seem aloof, including their use of the English language, made them eminently employable. Today's young Anglo-Indians are a far more confident lot and believe they have a greater stake in India. The skill sets are the same, but the mindsets have changed, both internally and externally.

For me, the message is clear enough: if you want a happy minority, create a happy society, with opportunity, hope and aspiration for everybody. If you construct a society with paranoia, pessimism and deprivation, you will not have a happy people and never a happy minority.

* * *

Nellie was a strong woman. In the mid-1940s, during the Great Calcutta Killings and the pre-Partition riots, she would walk down by the railway lines, from Sealdah to Ballygunge, tending to the injured. She was never harmed, not by Hindus and not by Muslims. The stethoscope around her neck established her credentials; the determined walk established her purpose. She would not be stopped, she would not be moved.

Nellie Bella O'Brien died at the ripe old age of seventy-eight in 1969. She was surrounded and mourned by her children, grandchildren and great-grandchildren. All of Jamir Lane, it seemed, turned out for her funeral. She wasn't just my father's grandmother, she was everybody's. The only one missing was Patrick, the son the mother had not seen for twenty-three years.

In 1984, my brother Andy, then a sports journalist, travelled to Karachi for hockey's Champions Trophy. He was determined to trace the lost O'Briens of Pakistan. He found them eventually and renewed contact. My father's uncle was dead, but the rest of the family was still there and greeted their Indian cousin very warmly. Most of my father's generation and all of the next generation—my second cousins—had converted to Islam. The pressure had been too much. Being a minority in Pakistan was tough business.

Andy came home and told us the strange and sombre story of the Muslim Anglo-Indian clan of Lahore and Karachi. We sat in silence, still digesting it. I thought of our life in India, the freedom to go to church, the freedom to practise my faith, the freedom to be myself, the freedom that my country gave its minorities. I've never felt prouder of being an Indian.

* * *

Postscript

Sometimes we don't realize how emotions lie within us, bottled up for years and decades. One day they burst out, in the most unlikely circumstances. It happened to me in August 2016, during a discussion in the Parliament on the turbulence in the Kashmir Valley. I had prepared my points, which were related to the manner in which the protests had been mishandled by the government.

That morning, just before leaving home, I glanced at the newspaper and read an obnoxious and offensive statement by a Pakistani diplomat, mocking and criticizing India for how it treated Kashmiris and religious minorities. That news report and the language the Pakistani official used stayed with me in the car. It rankled somewhere deep inside.

In the House, I was called to speak. I made my points as planned and finished with the last line I had in mind. I was about to sit down and the chairperson was about to call the next speaker, when I straightened up and stood erect again. Impromptu, completely on the spur of the moment, I felt I had to respond to that Pakistani official quoted in the news report. Even I don't know where those words came from:

Finally, some straight talk for our friends in Pakistan. Please don't meddle in our internal affairs. Please don't shed crocodile tears. Please don't pretend you have any love for the people of Kashmir. Please don't give my country any bogus lectures on pluralism and democracy. I say this with authority because my family knows Pakistan and my family knows India.

In 1947, when my grandfather and his younger brother worked in Kolkata (then Calcutta), the third brother was in Lahore, and he chose to stay there. Today, in spite of all the differences, in spite of all the problems we face, we are still the O'Briens of India. We can eat what we want. We can pray wherever we want to. We can walk the streets freely. But the O'Briens of Pakistan don't exist any more. They were forced to convert many years ago, and conform to a stereotype the Pakistani establishment prefers.

This is not a demand India has made of me. India and the Indian system, with all its problems and shortcomings, has been fair to me, to minorities, to minor minorities and to a variety of peoples and ethnicities and communities and regional identities. India has embraced all of these; given place under the sun to all of these to flourish and to prosper and to live with dignity. The people of Kashmir deserve as much. They deserve no more, and they deserve no less.

I sat down in a daze. It had been a short but emotionally wrenching intervention. A parliamentary colleague asked me if I was all right. I reached for a glass of water. Others both congratulated me for my closing remarks and said they had rarely found me so passionate. I smiled a weak smile.

Those were my words, I should have said, but this wasn't my script. It was Nellie's life, legacy and tragedy. I wasn't addressing the House that day, I was addressing Nellie—Nellie Bella O'Brien: mother of Amos of India and Patrick of Pakistan.

The Anti-colonial Origins of the Idea of India

MUKUL KESAVAN

Mukul Kesavan teaches history at Jamia Millia Islamia in Delhi. He has written a novel, *Looking through Glass*, a political tract, *Secular Common Sense*, and a book on cricket, *Men in White*. His most recent book is *Homeless on Google Earth*, a miscellany of columns and essays. He writes a weekly column for the *Telegraph*, Kolkata.

> Since the nineteenth century, India has played with two ideas of India: one that sought European-style nationhood built on uniformity; another that sought integration of minorities via recognition of diversities. Hindu nationalists have always sought the former; Gandhi and Nehru, whose ideas won out and were finally enshrined in the Constitution, thought accommodation of diversities would make minorities secure . . . They also thought that imposing uniformity would undermine India, not make it stronger. In India undifferentiated citizenship is an ideologue's or a philosopher's pipe dream with ghastly real-world implications.[1]

Varshney's characterization of Hindu and Congress nationalism is exactly right, specially his reference to the nineteenth-century origins of these rival nationalisms. The nationalism on which Gandhi and Nehru built, and which they stewarded into the

---

[1] Ashutosh Varshney, 'Why India Must Allow Hyphens', *Indian Express*, Delhi Edition, 2013, p. 13.

larger arenas of mass politics, had been constructed in the late nineteenth and early twentieth centuries by Congressmen who described themselves as Moderates.

They constructed an unusual nationalism based upon one presiding principle, the representation of diversity. It was a nationalism founded on a scrupulous recognition of India's heterogeneity, as opposed to the more characteristic nationalist strategy of trumpeting a unifying, homogenous identity.

It isn't hard to comprehend the reasoning and the historical logic behind self-strengthening movements amongst middle-class groups in late nineteenth-century India. The Muhammadan Anglo-Oriental College and Sir Syed Ahmad Khan, Bankim Chandra and the bhadralok are local examples of a widespread Asian response to colonial conquest and encroachment. Pankaj Mishra in *From the Ruins of Empire* takes us on a historical tour of intellectual responses to Western dominance in the Muslim world, in China, in Japan and in India.

Nor is it difficult to understand the impulse behind the indigenist cultural politics of Tilak, Aurobindo and Pal, Extremists all. They were adapting the homogenizing templates of European nationalism to Indian ends, high on sniffing those potent nationalist glues, religion and language.

Much more challenging (and historically relevant, given that the Moderate construction of Indian nationalism carried the day) is a historical explanation for the anti-majoritarian nationalism confected by Dadabhai Naoroji, Pherozeshah Mehta, Badruddin Tyabji, M.G. Ranade, Agarkar and Gokhale at the turn of the century. How did the colonial context of the Raj shape this eccentric political platform? What were the framing devices, the rhetorical conceits of this nationalism? How do we characterize it in the vocabulary of modern intellectual history?

The Origins of Congress Pluralism

Partha Chatterjee's choice of Bankim Chandra as the mascot of Indian nationalisms' 'moment of departure' is off by almost exactly a 1000 miles. The nationalism that eventually shaped and constituted the republic was nurtured across the breadth of the subcontinent in two Western Indian cities, Parsi Bombay and post-Peshwa Poona. If we are playing at making a list of the principal 'makers of modern India' or the makers of Congress nationalism, the shortlist of early makers would be the following: Dadabhai Naoroji, Pherozeshah Mehta, Dinshaw Wacha, Badruddin Tyabji, M.G. Ranade, Agarkar and Gopal Krishna Gokhale. In supporting roles we would have two Bengalis, R.C. Dutt and Surendranath Banerjea.

The obvious omission here is Tilak (and the other two in the triumvirate, Lajpat Rai and Bipin Chandra Pal), but they belong to another nationalist genealogy which *does* begin with Bankim and culminates in Bose, with Lal, Bal, Pal in the middle.

The Historical Context of Congress Nationalism

The argument here is that British India was reimagined as a nation in the last quarter of the nineteenth century. There were two rival ideas of India, one sponsored by the Moderates and the other by the Extremists, of which the former prevailed (though the latter remained alive as a dark alter ego, as Cain).

The nature of Moderate nationalism was determined by the interplay between certain givens—the sociological diversity of the subcontinent, the reality of direct centralized colonial rule over the subcontinent and the brutal and terrifying finality of the Raj's triumph in 1857. It was determined by the diversity, willingness, wit and ingenuity of a remarkable group of Western Indian public men to imagine the whole of the subcontinent as a nation in the making. It was determined by their ability to find the words, the arguments, the tricks and the representative manoeuvres that made the near-absurd audacity of this nationalist claim seem persuasive, even plausible.

Moderate nationalism's originality and peculiarity *all* relate to the challenge of credibly representing a very large (and *therefore* very diverse) population to both an alien sceptical Raj and the crazy quilt of communities that it claimed to represent.

The answers to this challenge that the Moderates returned weren't the only ones possible; Congress nationalism wasn't inevitably called into being by the nature of British colonialism. Savarkar's nationalist response to colonial rule was very different from that of Sir Pherozeshah Mehta's.

The reason Moderate ideology won out was because its substantive programme, its methods, its take on the politics of representation were more prudent, more pluralist, therefore more inclusive and rhetorically much less divisive and much more unifying than the alternatives on offer. The Moderates found a way of invoking an Indian nation without defining it culturally or at all; India was defined negatively as the sum of economic and political grievances of Queen Victoria's Indian subjects.

This section argues that the structure of Moderate nationalism, its rhetoric and its strategies were a durable legacy, that they went on to constitute the core principles of Gandhian nationalism and from there on to underwrite the pluralist principles of the Indian Constitution and to a lesser extent, the nature of the Indian republic, specially its politics.

The first principle of the Moderate or Congress ideology was a complete and unquestioning acceptance of the reality of the Raj and the fact that it was here to stay. The Raj was an immovable object and this had been proved beyond all doubt by the ruthless, near-demonic violence used to suppress the rebellion of 1857.

Historian Christopher Alan Bayly's argument that traditional patriotism seamlessly merged into modern nationalist politics, that the political ethics of the regional homelands survived and shaped the nature and reception of modern nationalism, doesn't seem persuasive. The Mutiny is a great rupture in colonial Indian history that buries a certain style of political resistance and the mythologies that supported and enabled it. There was no self-conscious way in which Maratha memories or manners could feed into post-1857 politics in Western India. 1857 was for Ranade, Mehta et al., the 'last war of imperial patriotism', not the 'first war of Indian independence'.

The first principle of Moderation, therefore, was not timorous caution but constitutionalist, non-violent engagement. From this side of 1857, violent resistance was doomed and any political flirtation with insurrectionary violence was, therefore, a sort of political infantilism. ' . . . the Bombay-based Indian social reformer in its editorials and columns consistently compared modern Indian history to European history after Napoleon, pointing to the manner in which the eruptions of 1848 in Europe or the emergence of Russian anarchist violence had actually impeded the movement towards constitutional government.'[2]

This taboo on political violence didn't extend to the Extremists. Again, in Bayly's words, '[T]he Maratha radicals lauded warrior sacrifice informed with knowledge while Tilak himself famously employed the Gita subtly to advocate the productive nature of political violence.'[3] Gandhian non-violence has, if not a lineal ancestor, a close cousin in the constitutionalist decorum of the Moderates, in their rejection of violent resistance or rebellion.

In Western India, the nursery of Moderate politics, the futility of violent rebellion against colonialism had been demonstrated three times: in 1844 in Kolhapur, where Shivaji's distaff descendants tried, unsuccessfully, to rally the Deccan Chiefs; in 1857 in Satara, when, in the wake of the Great Rebellion, there was an abortive attempt at *svarajya*; and finally in 1879, again in Satara, when a disaffected clerk, Vasudev Balwant Phadke, proclaimed himself the pradhan of Shivaji II. Our last rebel was sentenced to penal transportation for life and died in Aden. No one was foolish enough to rise again.[4]

---

[2] Christopher Bayly, *Recovering Liberties: Indian Thought in the Age of Liberalism and Empire*, Cambridge University Press, 2011, p. 266.

[3] Ibid.

[4] Stanley Wolpert, *Tilak and Gokhale: Revolution and Reform in the Making of Modern India*, Oxford University Press, 1990, pp. 8-9.

If the first premise of Moderate ideology was the permanence of the colonial presence and the self-destructiveness of violent resistance, its other defining feature was its imagining of an all-India nationalism. The nation that these early nationalists spoke for was coextensive with the boundaries of the British Raj. This seems unremarkable now, but it wasn't a given then. Bayly has persuasively argued for the historical significance of traditional provincial patriotisms, and as late as 1900, Ranade, Gokhale's mentor, could dream of the Maratha nation of the Peshwas finding a place under the Imperial sun in a federated India.

> . . . the remnants of the Confederacy that are still in the enjoyment of subordinate independence at Gwalior, Indore, Baroda, Kolhapur, Dhar and Dewas, the Southern Maratha Chiefs, and the Maratha population of about thirty millions included in the Bombay Presidency and the Native States, as also in the Central Provinces, Berar and the Nizam country, represent a power which is second to none among the native communities and States, which enjoy the protection of, and owe allegiance to, the British Rule. This element of present influence cannot also fail to have a deep interest to those who can see far into the future of the possibilities open to a Federated India, *distributed according to nationalities* [emphasis added] and subjected to a common bond of connection with the Imperial Power of the Queen-Empress of India.[5]

---

[5] Mahadev Govind Ranade, Verinder Grover (ed.), *Rise of the Maratha Power*, Abhijeet Publications, 2014, p. 154.

Gokhale, Ranade's disciple, but younger than him by a generation, would never have envisaged a Maratha nation within a loosely federated subcontinent—for him, born in 1866, the nationalist arena was pan-Indian in a politely anti-colonial way; not a federal aggregate of originary nations, such as that of the Marathas.

The very term 'all-India' is interesting: it indicates the strenuous determination not to be regional or provincial, the effort to house the diversity of the subcontinent in one nation.

This pan-Indianism was ideological, that is, it was constructed, deliberate, self-conscious, not some spontaneous emanation. The centralization of Imperial administration, the increasingly uniform subcontinental structures of colonial rule (the civil service, uniform legal codes, transport systems, the army) that characterized the Raj, the great subcontinental surveys, especially the census, the cartographic representations of the subcontinent as one political sovereignty, did supply contexts and reasons for thinking of India as a single political unit. So it could be argued that the nationalist imagination was shaped by the all-India sinews of the Raj; it was, in a fundamental way, a *colonial* nationalism.

The all-India imprint of the Raj shouldn't be underestimated: no regional nationalism challenged all-India imaginings till after 1947. The Pakistan movement and the party that led it, was inevitably called the All-India Muslim League and while the Dravida movement got its start in colonial India, its secessionist impulse in republican India remained feeble and muted.

So the imagining of India after 1857 necessarily involved the demotion of traditional patria into provincial franchises of an overarching Indian nation. This was common to both Extremist and Moderate nationalism, but much more thoroughgoing with the latter as Moderates tried to sidestep a culturalist nationalism that is a pan-Indian nationalism premised on the unifying properties of language or religion.

Having made the 'all-India' leap, Extremist leaders invoked a tolerant majoritarianism as the justification for the subcontinental claims. The census diversity of India, so different from the religious and linguistic sameness of more compact European nationalisms, was to be subordinated to the homogenizing history of an essentially Hindu People.

The Moderates, on the other hand, read the census reports, marvelled at the diversity of human kind arrayed in the Durbar of 1877 and arrived at a much odder and more complex nationalist politics. They accepted, in part, the colonial harping on difference, without accepting that this made democratic politics impossible in India. It spurred the Moderates to found the Congress (the Indian National Congress was a Moderate invention) as the embodiment of a literally representative politics. Which is to say that the Congress, both in its name and its composition, was to be more than a nationalist party; it was to be a representative assembly of desis, a Parliament-in-waiting that represented in its membership every constituency in this diverse subcontinent; these constituencies being read as communities of every sort, defined by a bouquet of criteria: language, religion, region, race . . .

The Congress pioneered a zoological nationalism where every Indian human species would be represented. The Congress was that odd nationalist vessel: it was Noah's ark, with two of every sort on board. This curating of diversity, this Noah's ark nationalism wasn't only pluralist idealism. It was also prudential.

The Congress needed to be inclusive to plausibly represent all-India to a hostile and sceptical Raj which had a reasonable claim to having authored the political unit that the Congress was now grandly invoking as its political constituency.

It is worth repeating that the durability of India, the number and variety of its people, was not remarkable in itself. Europe in any projection but Mercator's is, like India, a peninsular subcontinent, jutting off the Western end of the Asian land mass. It is every bit as various as British India was, but this variety was unremarkable whereas India's was remarked upon because Congress nationalism tried and substantially succeeded in assembling this diversity into a nation.

It is this adventure in assemblage/assembly that makes Congress (or Moderate) nationalism interesting, not merely its audacity in imagining a subcontinental nation. The Extremists claimed all of British India for Mother India but in much more conventional and derivative ways. Caste, language and religious differences were subsumed by a Hindu historicism and the invocation of a sublime Hindu-ness that tinctured every square of India's social quilt, even the green Muslim patches. Like the nationalists of that other giant state, the Russian Empire, an ineffable racial/religious/cultural unity negated, marginalized or subordinated apparent differences. Slavonic descent and the Orthodox Church were to Russian nationalists what the 'Aryan' heritage and the Sanatan Dharma were to Hindu nationalists of the Extremist sort. The care and scruple with which Moderates avoided majoritarian rhetoric and created a novel nationalism predicated on a pluralism that celebrated diversity is what makes Indian nationalism distinctive and interesting.

The Roots of Moderate Pluralism

Why were Moderate leaders like Gokhale and Naoroji mindful of India's diversity and concerned to build a self-consciously pluralist nationalism that represented that diversity? Conversely, why were Extremists careless of this diversity and insensitive to the implications of a majoritarian nationalism in a diverse subcontinent?

The answer isn't complicated. The Extremists spoke for an Indian nation that they assumed already existed, while Moderates like Gokhale implicitly believed that this nation needed to be constructed. Fired by the romantic nationalism of nineteenth-century Europe, the Extremists embraced the idea of self-determination, certain that the 'self' in question was a given. 'Svarajya', thundered Tilak, 'is my birthright and I shall have it.' The Indian self struggling for sovereignty was necessarily Hindu, forged out of the language, religion, culture and history of Hindus. Tilak's nationalism was implicitly majoritarian, it was a nationalism brewed out of Hindu Pad-Padashahi, Shivaji's proto-patriotic precedent and a certainty that Hindu mobilization was the key to a powerful nationalism. If these largely Hindu masses could be mobilized, nationalist demands would become irresistible and the colonial state would be forced to yield. The Moderates were deluded because they believed in the good faith of the Raj and the fantasy of a nation built out of colonial concessions.

The Extremists saw no reason to persuade the Raj of their nationalist credentials since they weren't looking for concessions, nor did they feel the need to perform pluralism because their nationalism pivoted on the idea of a Hindu People. This was a benevolent Hindu People, accommodative of non-Hindus, but in no way dependent on their approval. To read Tilak, B.C. Pal, Lajpat Rai and Aurobindo is to meet time and time again this Hindu nationalism which to them is coterminous with Indian nationalism with a cursory nod at Muslims and the others.

Tilak would have it that the Extremists and Moderates were agreed on the badness of the British rule, and that Extremists were merely the more militant, more advanced, more impatient vanguard of the same nationalism. Thus:

> Two new words have recently come into existence with regard to our politics, and they are *Moderates* and *Extremists*. These words have a specific relation to time and they, therefore, will change with time. The Extremists of today will be Moderates tomorrow, just as the Moderates of today were Extremists yesterday. When the National Congress was first started and Mr Dadabhai's views, which now go for Moderates, were given to the public, he was styled an Extremist, so that you will see the term Extremist is an expression of progress. We are Extremists today and our sons will call themselves Extremists and us Moderates. Every new party begins as Extremists and ends as Moderates.[6]

This is misleading. The Extremists represented a different type of nationalism from the politics of the Moderates. The difference

---

[6] Tilak Speech, 2/1/1907, *Bal Gangadhar Tilak: His Writings and Speeches*, pp. 37-52, collected in *Makers of Modern India,* Ramachandra Guha (ed.), Viking, Penguin Books India, Delhi 2010, p. 121.

between them was not a difference of degree of urgency, it was the unbridgeable gulf between a majoritarian nationalism borrowed from Central European templates and a pluralist nationalism improvised to earn representative credibility in the context of formal colonial rule.

The twenty years from the foundation of the Congress in 1885 to the temporary triumph of Extremism in 1905 in the form of the Swadeshi movement constitute a period where the Moderates constructed or tried to construct a consensual nationalism that could credibly claim to speak for a subcontinent's diverse people (with a small 'p'). It is a time when Congressmen like Naoroji and R.C. Dutt develop an economic critique of colonial rule that becomes the main plank of nationalist grievance, what C.A. Bayly calls statistical liberalism and Bipan Chandra, more appropriately, describes as economic nationalism.

This is best understood as a policy wonk's nationalism, the instrumentalist use of data for political ends. Tilak acknowledges the Moderate hand in the critique but still dismisses Naoroji, Gokhale et al. for their deluded timorousness, their misplaced trust in British good faith, their inability to understand the exploitative self-interest of colonial rule, their failure to see that nationalism had to be an uncompromising bid for sovereignty because only sovereignty brought political power, without which nationalist striving was a charade.

> If there is no svarajya there is no use labouring for the spread
> of female education, there is no use trying to secure industrial
> development and social reform can avail but little . . . Power

is the primary necessity and where there is power, there alone resides wisdom; wisdom never resides apart from power.[7]

That last sentence epitomizes the gulf between Tilak and Gokhale. In stark contrast to Tilak's will to power, the Moderates saw the Indianization of the Raj as central to nationalist assertion. They sought to influence colonial administration and policy to better serve Indian interests and welfare. They assumed or took for granted the fact that independence was a distant dream; what they sought were progressive steps towards self-government and policies that protected Indian economic interests. Unlike Tilak, they absolutely believed that incremental progress could be made without sovereignty. They believed that 'counter-preaching', to use Bayly's phrase, could delegitimize Anglo-Indian rule by slow degrees.

The Gandhian Congress is a peculiar meld of Extremist and Moderate ideas. Gandhi borrows boycott and non-cooperation and organization from Tilak. He borrows a distaste for the masculinist, militant, metaphorically violent rhetoric from Gokhale as also a willingness to work the councils.

Most of all, Moderates believed that this entryist strategy, this subversion from within, could only work if they carried the diversity of desis with them, else they would be outflanked by a sceptical Raj.

Put another way, the gradualism of the Moderates wasn't a function of timorousness or self-delusion; it was a necessary

---

[7] Ramachandra Guha (ed.), *Makers of Modern India*, Viking, Penguin Books India, Delhi 2010, p. 118.

consequence of their pluralism, their intuition that in the context of formal colonialism and a diverse empire, the right to speak for India had to be carefully, tactfully won, that an Indian nationalist politics had to be improvised because the mantras of European nationalisms didn't meet the subcontinental case. Mother India, in short, couldn't be squeezed into the petticoats of smaller European women.

So the Extremists weren't 'advanced' nationalists measured by some simple yardstick of radicalism or militancy or political urgency. They weren't Moderates on steroids. They were political beasts of an entirely different sort, namely Hindu nationalists. This can be simply illustrated. There are *no* Extremists who aren't Hindu. Tilak, Lajpat Rai, B.C. Pal, Aurobindo, the revolutionary terrorists of the Swadeshi movement, every single member of the Extremist faction was ascriptively Hindu. This is not surprising: the iconography, language, invented traditions, mobilizational idiom of Extremism is so suffused with Hinduism that it would have been impossible for a non-Hindu to participate without actually converting to Hinduism as Sister Nivedita did or something close to it, like the Theosophists.

Forget being born Hindu, there are no Extremist leaders who are politically radical without being politically Hindu; that is to say, there are no Extremists who articulate militancy, radicalism and urgency in a secular way. The point of this is to discount the notion that Extremism is defined principally by the vanguardist nationalism of its adherents; what Extremists had in common was militant identitarian politics, not a more robust patriotism.

One reason for the Moderate-controlled Congress's success in resisting this temptation was its keenness on Muslim support;

the other was the Congress's great good fortune in being led both intellectually and organizationally by Parsis in the first twenty years of its existence.

The Parsis and the Bombay Gharana

Dadabhai Naoroji, Pherozeshah Mehta and Dinshaw Wacha epitomized in their different ways the early Congress. If Naoroji was the oldest member, the Grand Old Man, the pioneer of economic nationalism and the Congress's voice in England for decades, Pherozeshah Mehta and his friend Dinshaw Wacha were Moderate enforcers, determined to keep the Congress on the straight and narrow of constitutionalist politics and out of the Hindu populist hands of Tilak and his henchmen. Rather like the pioneering role Parsis played in domesticating cricket, they also established the first principles of Congress nationalism.

The Parsis were a successful minority that, having prospered in trade, industry and the Western professions had a stake in the colonial state and a determination to work this structure on level terms. Westernized Anglophiles, they were concerned with equality in the professions and in business and saw politics as a series of briefs about policy. Crucially, not being Hindu, they were immune to the lure of revivalist Hindu politics or indeed any form of politics that disrupted the transactional order of the Raj.

But the Parsis shouldn't be seen as compradors. Pherozeshah Mehta was a man of enormous professional and political consequence in Bombay. He had served four terms as the chairman of the Bombay corporation, three terms as a member of the Imperial Legislative Council where he ruffled the Anglo-Indian bureaucracy. His ' . . . blunt criticisms of government policies angered English members who denounced him for the "new spirit" he had introduced. In 1901, he led a walkout of five Indian members from the Bombay Legislative Council to protest the manner in which the officials on the council treated their efforts to amend a land revenue bill. Moderate though he was, he was no mendicant.'[8]

Naoroji was even more influential. He, along with R.C. Dutt, authored the economic critique of colonial rule that was to be Congress's stock-in-trade through its anti-colonial career. Thanks to them, the Congress's nationalism wasn't founded on fantasies of cultural hurt and healing. Naoroji was India's first British MP and, perhaps more importantly, mentor to Pherozeshah Mehta, Badruddin Tyabji, W.C. Bonnerjee, Manmohan Ghose, R.C. Dutt, all of whom were Moderates and all of whom had been members of Naoroji's London Indian Society, founded in 1865. He was an inspiration to M.G. Ranade, K.T. Telang and William Wedderburn. In age he was to help the Congress and the Moderates to selectively appropriate militant demands like Swaraj without the culturalist baggage that the Extremists had coloured them with. Naoroji was happy to lend his distinction to Besant's Home Rule League towards the end of his life.

By helping to create an economic and progressive critique of colonial rule and by cordoning off the Congress from the Hindu

---

[8] John Mclane, *Indian Nationalism and the Early Congress*, Princeton University Press, 1977, p. 167.

excesses of militant politics, the Parsis stamped the Congress with a secular and pluralist watermark which successfully saw off the Extremist challenge. The triumph of the Moderates was substantially a Parsi triumph and it was a historic victory because it made majoritarianism, the default mode in the history of European nationalisms, a bad word in Indian nationalist politics.

The Moderates are in *this* sense (as the founders of an anti-majoritarian nationalism) best seen as the Bombay Gharana founded by Naoroji, its guru, whose disciples, or *shishyas* included Ranade, Mehta, Tyabji, Wacha, Gokhale and, in an odd, mutated way, Gandhi.

The Bombay Gharana was essentially a Parsi school with the odd Chitpavan or Bohra or Bengali thrown in. If it hadn't been for the singular context of Bombay, a city that had hothoused an assertive Indian capitalist elite made up of culturally and religiously diverse trading communities, the most important of them being the Parsis, there would have been no anti-majoritarian nationalism, no self-consciously pluralist Moderate faction, no Congress ideology.

Calcutta couldn't have hosted the Moderates. Despite Manmohan Ghose, Lalmohan Ghose, Surendranath Banerjea and R.C. Dutt, Calcutta's nationalist politics was essentially Extremist, a cultural nationalism that derived from Bankim Chandra's mother-smothered effusions. It is revealing that R.C. Dutt and Surendranath Banerjea, the two principal Moderate leaders from Bengal, shared with the Extremists a historicism that joined the Indian nation to an essentially Hindu past. It's tempting to argue that a bhadralok made up of absentee Hindu zamindars, alienated from both the Muslim tenantry that they mulcted for rent and a precolonial political history made up of 'Muslim' states, sought self-esteem and reassurance in stirring retellings of a Hindu history. R.C. Dutt's novels saw India's principal economic historian wallowing in revivalist fantasies of India's past, while Banerjea wrote an essay, 'The Study of History', in which he urged the study of Indian history as a way of discovering its glorious, entirely Hindu past.

Without the Bombay Gharana the Moderates would have merely been the more timorous faction of a standard-issue majoritarianism. Without the Parsis, the Moderates wouldn't have had a kernel of non-Hindu leaders who were immune to Hindu populist rhetoric.

The influence of the Parsis over Moderate and Congress nationalism should be understood in the context of a tiny public world that was dominated by small elites. The Parsi influence on this world was entirely out of proportion to the size of the community. Just as the Bombay Quadrangular, a cricket tournament, included a Parsi XI pitted against a Hindoo XI and a Mahomedan XI with no sense of demographic incongruity, so too were influential Parsis an elite equal or superior to Muslim or Hindu or Bengali or Madrasi elites.

The importance of being Parsi was that, existentially, Naoroji, Wacha and Mehta were incapable of backsliding into majoritarianism simply because they belonged to a tiny demographic minority. Their Parsi being, the identity they inherited, negatively shaped their political commitments by ruling out certain ideological positions.

It wasn't as if Parsis were predisposed to empathy towards Muslims. On the contrary—both as Zoroastrians with a historical memory of being expelled from Iran by the political armies of the Khilafat and as wealthy professionals and businessmen in a city with a large Muslim underclass—Parsis often found themselves opposed to sections of Muslims.

For example, Pherozeshah Mehta wasn't held back by political correctness when he described his experience of anti-Parsi Muslim rioters in Bombay in 1874:

> . . . our buggy was surrounded by the rioters shouting and yelling at us, as if the very sight of a Parsee was a sort of red flag to them and we were assailed with a perfect storm of missiles . . . we were compelled to bring out a gun and two revolvers which we had taken care to provide ourselves with before starting. The effect was electric; like the veriest dastards that they really were, the very sight of fire-arms sent them flying in all directions, clearly proving to us that only a bold front and a firm hand were required to quell this beggarly rabble and scum of the Mahomedan population.[9]

It wasn't as if ideological pluralism was a peculiar characteristic of the Parsis; it is their willingness to assert themselves as Indian notables, *raises* in Sir Syed's usage, immune to the

---

[9] From *Pherozeshah Mehta* (vol. 1, 84) by Homi Mody cited in John Mclane, *Indian Nationalism and the Early Congress*, Princeton University Press, 1977, p. 70.

blandishments of Hindu nationalism that makes them significant in the history of nationalism. At a crucial stage in the Congress's early history, the Bombay Gharana held the pass against a majoritarian, 'culturalist' politics which, otherwise, would have seemed utterly normal, thanks to the prestige of European histories of nationalism which took majoritarian national identity for granted.

Parsis counted for very little, politically, after the Congress split at Surat in 1907. With the Morley-Minto reforms of 1909 and the era of mass politics inaugurated by Gandhi, they count for nothing at all. But before politics became a matter of numbers, through the twenty years between 1885 and 1905 when politics consisted of grandees ventriloquizing for an offstage India, they kept out of the way of Hindu populists like Tilak and Pal and Aurobindo; they forged an indigenous pluralism for the Congress in its formative years. So when Gandhi took hold of the Congress and launched it into mass politics, he inherited a political vessel unfreighted with Hindu nationalism. Gandhi was heir to a pluralist nationalism and his task was to keep this pluralism afloat on the stormier and more challenging seas of mass politics.

The inclusiveness that defined anti-colonial nationalism at its best had a curious history: it was fathered by the constraints of colonialism, a well-founded anxiety about the Congress's claim to represent India, the elitism of early nationalist politics and an idealistic, deeply felt commitment to accommodating difference. The Congress's awareness that turning a subcontinent into a nation, a delicate, complex business, was hard-won; it was a knowledge born out of its experience of the anti-colonial struggle. It was no coincidence, then, that the constituent assembly created, despite Partition, a scrupulously secular republic which refused the temptation of sameness and chose to embody the diversity of this unprecedented nation.

India: From Identity to Freedom

PRATAP BHANU MEHTA

Pratap Bhanu Mehta, the vice chancellor of Ashoka University, has written extensively on political theory, constitutional law and politics in India. His most recent publication is *The Oxford Handbook to the Indian Constitution*, co-edited with Madhav Khosla and Sujit Choudhury. He is the recipient of the Infosys Prize, 2011. Mehta is also a regular columnist for the *Indian Express*.

What I want to do in this essay is to revisit a very old question, that in its modern forms Indians have debated at least since 1857. The question I am going to be posing is an old one in political theory: the tension between individual and group rights. But rather than taking a philosophical route to this question, I want to pose a stylized contrast between two different ways in which the question of the relationship between the individual and the group has played out in two contrasting ideas of India, or more precisely, the terms in which Indians relate to each other.

I shall call these two imaginings of India a 'Federation of Communities' and 'India as a Zone of Freedom' respectively. The deeper, but unarticulated, battle in India is not between secularism and communalism as conventionally understood, important as that battle is. It is, rather, a battle between two different ideas of India: Is India a federation of communities (FOC) or a zone of individual freedom (ZIF)? In our political culture, the idea that India is a federation of communities has become almost inescapable common sense, in a way that poses a great threat to liberty and distorts our intellectual culture. Both ideas rest on variants of the idea of toleration, but their underlying logic is different.

The purpose of drawing this contrast is threefold. First, to argue that despite superficial similarities there is a deep tension between these two ideas and that many of the pathologies of our politics can be traced to the tension between them. The second is to make a point about Indian intellectual history. Our conventional ways of thinking about the central tension between secularism and communalism are, I will argue, deeply misleading. Our conventional classifications of major figures in Indian intellectual history, based on this divide, often present a misleading picture of what is at stake. And the third is to shed some light on the nature of conflicts being played out in contemporary India. Though we will come to this only briefly towards the end.

The Dead Ends of Diversity

So let me begin by sketching, in bold strokes, the picture of India as a federation of communities. In this view, India is a diverse country, a bewildering mosaic of communities of all kinds; its peculiar genius is to fashion a form of coexistence where this diversity can flourish and find its place. It has created cultures of political negotiation that have shown a remarkable ability to incorporate diversity.

This description of India is often exhilarating; and it is our dominant mode of self-presentation. But its very attractiveness hides its deep problems. The problem lies with the normative valorization of diversity itself. Diversity is something to be celebrated and cherished for often it is an indication of other values like freedom and creativity. But diversity has become a source of several intellectual confusions. Very schematically these are: Diversity is not itself a freestanding moral value. It makes very little sense to discuss diversity as carrying independent moral weight, even though under some circumstances, loss of diversity can be an indication of other underlying injustices. The invocation of diversity immediately invites the question: Diversity of what? This question cannot be answered without invoking some normative criteria about the permissible range of social practices. The limits to diversity cannot themselves be settled by an invocation of diversity.

The appeal to diversity is usually an aestheticized appeal. It is as if one were surveying the world from nowhere and contemplating this extraordinary mosaic of human cultural forms and practices. Such a contemplation of the world can give enormous enrichment and satisfaction and we feel that something would be lost; perhaps something of humanity would be diminished if this diversity were lost. But the trouble is that this view from nowhere, or if you prefer an alternative formulation, the 'God's Eye' view of the world is a standpoint of theoretical, not practical, reason.

Most of us can conceptually grasp the fact of diversity; we may even try to recognize each other in an intense and important way, but it is very difficult to live that diversity with any degree of seriousness. From this theoretical point of view, cultures and practices form this extraordinary mosaic;

from the practical point of view of those living within any of these cultures, these cultures and practices are horizons within which they operate. Even when not oppressive, these horizons might appear to them as constraints. It would be morally obtuse to say to these individuals that they should go on living their cultures, just because their not doing so might diminish the forms of diversity in the world. The imperatives of diversity cannot, at least prima facie, trump the free choices of individuals.

There is often a real tension between the demands of integration into wider society—the imperatives of forming thicker relationships with those outside the ambit of your own society on the one hand, and the measures necessary to preserve a vibrant cultural diversity on the other. What the exact trade-off is depends from case to case. But simply invoking diversity by itself will not help morally illuminate the nature of the decision to be made when faced with such a trade-off.

From this perspective, talk of identity and diversity is profoundly misleading because it places value on the diversity of cultures, not the freedoms of individuals within them. If the range of freedom expands, all kinds of diversity will flourish anyway. But this will not necessarily be the diversity of well-defined cultures. It will be something that both draws upon culture and subverts it at the same time.

Diversity Talk is compatible with only one specific conception of toleration: segmented and hierarchical toleration. To be fair, India has been remarkably successful at providing a home for all kinds of groups and cultures. But each group could find a place because each group had its fixed place. To put it very schematically, it was a form of toleration compatible with walls between communities. Indeed, one of the major challenges for Indian society is that we have internalized forms of toleration that are suited to segmented societies. It is compatible with the idea that boundaries should not be crossed, populations should not mix, and that to view the world as a competition between groups is fine.

There is no country in the world that talks so much of diversity. Yet no other country produces such a suffocating discourse of identity; where who you are seems to matter at every turn: what job you can get, what government scheme you are eligible for, how much institutional autonomy you can get, what house you can rent. Conceptually, there is no incompatibility between celebrating diversity of the nation and refusing to rent housing to a Muslim just because they are Muslim. Such a conception of toleration does not work where the need is for boundaries to be crossed: people will inhabit the same spaces, compete for the same jobs, intermarry and so forth. Our moral discourse is so centred on diversity and pluralism that it forgets the more basic ideas of freedom and dignity.

Diversity is also compatible with philosophical non-engagement. I was teaching two texts back to back: Iqbal's dazzling book, *The Reconstruction of Religious Thought in Islam*, and Sri Aurobindo's ambitious *The Human Cycle*. One of the questions emerging from the discussion was this: These are works of breathtaking ambition. They have a philosophy of history, they deeply engage with Western thinkers like Nietzsche and

Bergson, they synthesize reason with other aspects of the human personality, and they wrestle with questions of community and humanity. They engage with the whole world. But they do not engage the traditions adjacent to them. It is almost as if, except for a cursory reference to idolatry, Hindu thought does not exist for Iqbal; and Islam does not for Aurobindo. This is all the more surprising because the philosophical ground they occupied, a discussion of Being and Reason, could have been amenable to such a dialogue. After all, both are talking to Nietzsche. Aurobindo was later to say that he could have engaged with Islam if he knew Persian, and that Sufi philosophy could perhaps provide a philosophical meeting ground. Sufism was of course, precisely the philosophical stance Iqbal criticized. But the larger puzzle is this: Why despite an extraordinary coexistence of Hinduism and Islam, is their mutual philosophical engagement so meagre? Carl Ernst has laboriously documented Persian translations of yoga and other texts; and there are scattered references to Islamic thinking in Sanskrit texts. But the scale of deep conceptual engagement has remained surprisingly modest on all sides. Whatever the engagement between Hinduism and Islam at the vernacular level, at the level of philosophical thought, these were like the banks of two rivers, running parallel, but not destined to meet.

There is of course one major exception to this that involves the first 'Varanasi' project. This was Dara Shikoh's working with Banaras Pandits to translate, amongst other things, all the Upanishads. Much can be written about Dara Shikoh's enterprise. But two claims about it were striking. The first, as Ganeri points out, was the deep philosophical engagement: The Upanishads were to be used to interpret and reveal the truth of the Quran. The second claim, embodied in his masterwork, *Majma-al-Baharain* (The Meeting of Two Oceans), was the mutual reinterpretation of Islam and Hinduism in terms of each other's categories. But this was not, as modern shallow understandings often portray, a political gesture synthesizing two traditions. The meeting of the two oceans was meant to refer to the instant where a moment of Enlightenment is produced. It is an intellectual engagement not driven by a desire to add identities, but to transcend them in the name of knowledge. This is perhaps the spirit that led the French observer Bernier to describe Varanasi at the time as the Athens of the East, the place where all kinds of cross-currents circulated. One central figure who plays a big role in this story, who Bernier seems to have consulted, is the great Kavindracharya Saraswati, patronized by a Dara Shikoh acolyte, Danishmand Khan. No wonder, the Sanskrit scholar P.K. Gode could write this about seventeenth-century India, 'It was a tie of learning that brought together a Frenchman of Paris, a Muslim of Persia and a Brahmin of Banaras, actuated by only the motive of learning of thought which we so value in modern times.' But in a sense these were the exceptions that proved the rule. In short, diversity can also be compatible with forms of non-engagement. Now there might be a certain intellectual humility in these forms of non-engagement, no presumptuous claim to possess the 'Other', but often it has also created a persistent distance.

In short, diversity talk can be quite compatible with a non-recognition of freedom.

The Dead Ends of Identity

If diversity has obscured rather than enhanced the value of freedom, and produced a form of toleration less suited to the 'endosmosis' of modern society (a phrase adapted by Ambedkar from Dewey) it has done something even more insidious to our conceptions of identity. Identities matter to people. They should not be threatened for being who they are; they need ample space for self-discovery and expression of identity, and as expressions of freedom identities are to be cherished. But we have instituted what I might call the 'tyranny of compulsory identities', under the peculiar form of toleration we practise. Their compulsion makes them insidious. How have these identities become 'compulsory'? It has to be acknowledged that it is no surprise that a society that invented as oppressive a system of compulsory identities as caste will continue to be haunted by it. But the means through which we have sought to redress that ancient tyranny have reinvented compulsory identities in new forms. The problem is not the proliferation of identities; that may be a good thing. The problem is the assumption that these identities are inescapable.

These identities are inescapable legal categories. In a state where what rights you have, what marriage law you are governed by, what property rules you fall under, what institutions you can run all depend on the legal system classifying you in a particular category. So in this sense you cannot escape them, no matter what you want to make of yourself. This is not necessarily an argument for doing away with identity-based exemptions or allocations. In some cases, particularly for addressing historical injustice and continued deprivation some identity-based laws are essential. This is particularly the case for Dalits. But the alignment of identity and rights is far more widespread than required by a normative basis for justice.

The premise of enumeration is that we can never escape identity. Our identities are not something we can choose; they are given as non-negotiable facts which we can never escape. The state has legitimized the principle that we will always be our caste. This is a way of diminishing our freedom, agency and dignity in a way that even votaries of tradition could not dream of. It takes away the fundamental freedoms we need to define ourselves. Is there not a deeper indignity being inflicted on those to whom emancipation is being promised? You will be your caste, no matter what. There is a risk of gracelessness here. But we have too many purveyors for whom social justice is endless stratagem to assert the power of compulsory group identity, rather than finding the means to escape it. In the name of breaking open prisons, they imprison us even more.

The possibilities of self-definition in identities diminish. In a liberal society, your identity should be a matter of self-definition. Who you take yourself to be should be your choice. Answers to these questions should be entirely up to you. But the Indian state gives no choice in legal terms. It has created large categories into which everyone gets slotted, and then when those definitions do not satisfy all identities it creates new exemptions. But citizens can have a real choice about their own identities only when these identities do not affect what rights and privileges they will enjoy. For instance, the whole clamour for minority status stems largely from one issue: the right to administer one's own institutions without the state imposing its own norms. Minority status has become the identity equivalent of the exemption mania in taxation. We design bad tax policies and then give different groups special dispensations. The same is true of the state and freedom to institutions. Instead of simple rules that say people are free to run whatever kinds of institutions they wish to run, subject to certain minimal regulations, we have a legal structure that imposes draconian restrictions on institutions with respect to whom they can admit, how much they can charge, what they teach and how they are to be administered. There is a perception that minority institutions are often exempt from these requirements. A more 'secular' basis for protecting minority institutions without aligning citizenship and democracy is to give all communities the same freedom of association; the state regulates all equally, so long as it demonstrates some presumptive secular reason for doing so (for instance, the institution receives state funds). Similarly, when it comes to personal law, identity considerations of communities should be secondary. The sole relevant test needs to be: will the particular reform best express our standing as free and equal individuals within communities.

One conceptual move necessary to combat communal constructions is this. Every community, majority or minority, often appeals to the thought that something must not be imposed on them if they do not consent to it. The problem is that communities do not often extend the same courtesy to individuals within them. We have tied ourselves in knots trying to distinguish Indian secularism from its other variants, in castigating liberalism as a foreign ideology. But all that liberalism requires to get started is by extending the courtesy of the very same argument—that communities use to keep other communities out—to individuals within them. The freedom from another community cannot be the freedom to oppress within. As far as possible, we want to live under social arrangements that honour our standing as free and equal individuals. The battle in India is not between majorities and minorities. It is between forces and institutions in each community that want to bend the arc of history away from freedom and equality in the personal space, and forces that want to claim those rights. This is a contest that cuts across communities with varying degrees of intensity. But it is something of an own goal when secularists, rather than reconfiguring the debate, as one between freedom and equality on the one hand, and coercion and subordination on the other, also come to be invested in the contest of compulsory identities. The only way the long-term threat of majoritarianism can be dissolved is by moving the axis of contest away from the majority minority distinction, to equal protection of *individual* rights, freedom and dignity.

As Flavia Agnes, one of the most thoughtful and grounded contributors to this debate has pointed out, we must be wary of a lot of communal myth-making in this area. It is not only minorities who have been advocates of personal law. The Hindu Code Bill, with all its reform elements, was a sectarian reform aimed as much at consolidating a unified Hindu legal identity, as it was aimed at progressive social reform. Arguably the contractual framework for marriage in Islam can be more easily adapted to modern marriage laws than sacramental conceptions. Muslim personal law has also been subject to reform. Despite the cowardly abdication by the Congress in the Shah Bano affair, the Supreme Court has incrementally introduced reform, without opposition, it has to be said. (Most notably, in the Danial Latifi case). So, arguably, there is propitious grounds for serious, good faith conversation on the issue. The conversation has to be oriented to the future. For this reason, its sole concern has to be freedom, equality and justice, not nationalism or selective narratives of which community was more oppressive in the past. It is high time we rescued that conversation from being held hostage by three forces: bodies like the Muslim Personal Law Board that are non-representative and reactionary, Hindutva ideologies that are more interested in using the issue to demonize minorities than to expand the space for freedom, and some secularists whose politics of fear has given them an investment in war of identities rather than the expansion of rights.

The biggest identity threat to freedom comes in the form of nationalism. The most insidious way in which nationalism colonizes culture is by reversing an order of priorities. In the nationalistic view of culture a compelling reason for certain practices, beliefs or way of life is that these are *mine*. They are to be followed because they belong to a group, and make them what that group is. On this view there is an obligation to follow practices because of their origins, of the fact of possession, to defend them because they are ours. But while this thought provides impetus for culture, it also destroys it. For now, culture is no longer embedded in the space of reasons; it is driven by the imperatives of identity. They are defended not because they are good but because they are ours. Now this is not such a big problem, except when it is articulated so insistently in the public space. There is nothing more suffocating in Indian cultural criticism than to reduce culture to the question of origin. Often it is done in a well-meaning, benign way. But often it is part of an unthinking way in which we define other people's identities for them. Looking at individuals through the prism of group identity, whether they identify with it or not, also diminishes them. We are always more than who we are, we can always be different from what we are. But to excessively focus on individuals as being of interest because they represent some group, is to devalue individuals. Identity is a fact about us, but it should not define the horizon of our possibilities; we should celebrate people's achievements, not reward them for the identity they might have. We need to privilege freedom over identity to protect genuine diversity.

Take the very question, 'What is India'. This is a trap. It does not have a natural answer. It only exposes the fragility of any conception of identity. It will lead inevitably to a contest over an authoritative definition, which will be decided by those who have most power. Second, any process of creating an identity will lead to creating other identities. Indeed, the difficulty for most minorities in India at the current conjuncture is that their otherness is overdetermined. If we say that Indian identity is constituted by fidelity to a religion, they are excluded. If we say, as Savarkar did, that Indian identity is constituted by belonging to a single race, those who do not acknowledge that fact are excluded.

In short, every attempt to benchmark Indian identity, define it in terms of litmus tests, will produce mischief. I suspect Hindutva cannot be matched simply by counterposing some other conception of Indian identity. The problem is not simply Hindutva; Hindutva is made possible by a prior obsession with identity. Rather, the trick is to resist the allure of the identity question altogether.

Politically, what India needs is not so much a new conception of Indian identity, one that emphasizes pluralism and compositeness. Rather, what we need is a social contract over how we respect and deal with those with whom we disagree about India's identity. We don't need to ask, 'What do we share?' Rather we need to ask, 'What are the terms on which we relate to those with whom we disagree about what we share or with whom we share nothing at all?' The challenge is not to find something we share; the challenge is to find ways of acknowledging difference.

Does all this mean that India does not have an identity? If this demand implies that there is something we all unequivocally share, the answer is no. But it does not preclude the thought that we all have lots of different reasons and ways in which we define our relationships to one another. There is no 'unity' in diversity, rather we are diverse in our unities, and we might identify with connections to India, each in our own way. But any attempt to produce an authoritative conception of India will be fraught with exclusion and violence. We should take some heart from the fact that usually it does not occur to anybody to doubt whether India has an identity, until someone begins to give arguments to prove it.

I could go on. But what I hope to have convinced you of is that looking upon India as a federation of communities is premised on an impoverished conception of toleration, can be quite incompatible with freedom and leads to the tyranny of compulsory identities.

From Federation of Communities to Zone of Freedom

This is why India needs to move away from the idea that it is composed of a social contract between communities, to the idea that it should be a zone of individual freedom. The normative intuition is simply this: If we are committed to a single scale of moral judgement that derives from universal norms, it's a scale that slides all the way down. There is a paradox that afflicts all arguments for accommodative political community that depend on seeing themselves as federations of communities. These conceptions turn on the plausible thought that if the national identity is somehow 'thinner', demands less sacrifice from its constituent parts, and is open to continual and even far-reaching negotiation, it will allow for thicker sub-national identities or partial alternative sovereignties to flourish. But morally, there seems to be something odd about an argument that calls for the thinning of national identities so that other identities can flourish more thickly. Why shouldn't the sliding scale go all the way down again? If the argument is that no conception of identity should be imposed on others, it is presumably because it would be wrong to impose conditions on people that they could not freely accept. But *this* moral claim goes all the way down; all identities—national or otherwise—have to pass the tribunal of justificatory reasons. But it is difficult to imagine—at least if one takes moral individualism seriously—that this demand is compatible with thick identities that are collectively held or to which allegiance is given.

One of the lines of reasoning that lies behind giving different cultural communities their own space, even forums of representation, is that the demands that others 'outside' the community make could not be justified to *them*. But this is a demand that individuals within any culture or subculture can place upon their culture as well. In short, there is no escaping the burdens of justification. The demand that the reasons for the application of power be acceptable to those over whom power is exercised, is one that goes all the way down. It is a demand even individuals can make. But this has two consequences: the demand will be for political orders that protect the right to dissent, and the decreasing normative sovereignty of the claims of culture or partial identities to individuals within it.

So the claim that India should give primacy to individual freedom does not rest on any normative commitment to values like individualism. It does entail a moral individualism, in that the individual is the unit of moral justification. It takes no stand on what kinds of lives individuals might want to lead, whether these are ones of deracination or thick cultural belonging. All it says is that these should be freely chosen. And it applies the same argument that is used to see India as a federation of communities: nothing must be imposed upon communities that they would not accept.

On values, the FOC places primacy on group diversity. ZIF places primacy on individual freedom. ZIF values diversity, but as an outcome of free individuals exercising their choices. It rests on the intuition that the same moral rights that groups claim, namely that nothing should be imposed on them that they could reasonably object to, should be applied to all individuals within group as well.

On toleration, FOC is compatible with segmented toleration: each group has its rightful place, so long as it stays in its rightful place. This has been the traditional Indian conception of toleration, peculiarly ill-fitted to an age of mobility and competition within the same spaces: different groups will inhabit the same workplace, intermarry and so forth. ZIF recognizes that the challenge is not protecting community identities; it is protecting those who breach them.

On citizenship, FOC is premised on differentiated citizenship. What rights you have in particular areas depend upon your identity. This applies not just to areas of personal law, which are out of the purview of common deliberation. But these extend to matters like the right to administer institutions. The degree of autonomy an institution is allowed in education, for example, depends on its identity, not functionality or financial relation to the state. ZIF is premised on common citizenship as much as possible, and on the idea that rights and identity must not be as closely aligned as in FOC.

Both differ in approach to identity. FOC is enamoured by identities. Our legal identities are in part mediated by compulsory group identities. Our social and political interactions are premised on inescapably slotting people into identities; individuals are this 'case', that religion and so forth. There is no escaping this identity. ZIF acknowledges that people should not be targeted for being who they are; occasionally an axis of deprivation structured around identity may need to be addressed. But it finds the constant need to slot individuals into compulsory identities suffocating.

Both have a different approach to justice. In FOC, the primary metaphor for justice is representation and balancing. The distribution of power should match the distribution of identities. No matter what representatives do, they count as representatives of a particular community by virtue of ethnicity. The primary mode of politics is balancing; if one community is given something, another community must be given something in recompense. For ZIF, the primary metaphor for justice is equal opportunity for individuals. ZIF is suspicious of claims to represent, because it is suspicious that they are unified community claims that can be represented; what individuals do is more important than what group they stand for. In FOC, the emphasis is on a politics of overt symbolism that can serve the needs of balancing and representation. For ZIF, the emphasis is on institutions that can protect individual rights.

With these rough contrasts, the intellectual history of modern India looks quite different. Our Constitution's ambition was to convert India into a zone of freedom, to liberate individuals from the burden of compulsory identities, to create a common citizenship and to give primacy to individual rights. But it made a few compromises that allowed identity to become central to thinking about citizenship. But what the Constitution left as a tension, our political culture transformed into a full-scale advocacy of India as a federation of communities. For example, its conception of Indian citizenship was to think in terms of Hindu plus Muslim, not to think beyond Hindu and Muslim; it was to think in terms of a collection of castes, not beyond caste. And our existing social practice has deep affinity with this way of thinking. ZIF does not argue that these identities will vanish, only that they will be largely private matters.

In this framework, the intellectual history of Partition looks different. I want to make a little aside on the politics of representation and partition.

A political order can claim more justly to represent a people when the diverse constituencies within it are represented in the sense that the political order gives, or at any rate allows, full expression to their identities' needs and wants. Such representation allows more constituencies to feel at home in that political order, it enables them to think of this political order as, in some senses, their own. But in principle, the question of the representative relationship between the ruler and the ruled is somewhat independent of the question of what the political order as a whole represents.

But the formation of a representative political order of this kind turns on a paradox. The most formidable obstacles to creating representative democracy do not turn on the ill-posed question of democratic values, whether members of a particular society have the values in question (whether or not they can understand and respect supposedly complicated ideas like elections, voting and free discussion). The most formidable challenge turns out to be the trustworthiness of the structures of representation. Who does the political community represent? And the ensuing dilemma is that structures of representation can be most trusted when they are least tested by the burden of identities. It is a sobering thought that there is possibly not a single transition from imperial rule (or authoritarian rule more generally) that has not involved this identity quagmire. From India to Iraq, from Fiji to Sri Lanka, the structure of the dilemma is uncannily similar.

The introduction of representative government introduces a large question. How is this representation going to be organized? This question becomes more rather than less acute under conditions of universal suffrage. If there is a significant minority, with some legitimate vestment in its identity, it fears being swamped by simple numerical majority rules. It therefore seeks forms of representation that can protect its interests, or give expression to its identity. But here arises a dilemma. If they are given representation in excess of their numbers or some special protection, there is a fear of a majority backlash. The majority fears the entrenchment and institutionalization of what it thinks are unfair concessions to the minority. Their vestments in identity turn out to be at least in tension with the majority's vestments that the state be its own. Take for instance the case of pre-partition India.

What we think of as Hindu–Muslim politics in India was born squarely in the crucible of representative politics, and this has increasingly become an underappreciated fact. To simplify a complicated story for the purposes of illustration, Syed Ahmad Khan had early on sensed that the albeit gradual introduction of representative government might prove to be a threat to Muslims, because it would naturally advantage Hindus numerically. Thus began a complex debate over Muslim representation that was never quite solved. Various proposals were floated: separate electorates, the grouping of Muslim majority provinces and so forth. But, in retrospect, it is clear that no stable solution to this conundrum was forthcoming. Any 'extra' concessions to safeguard minority interests would provoke a backlash from some section of the Hindus. Why give Muslims representation in excess of their numbers? This was the crux of the Hindu Mahasabha's and the Congress's own Right wing's critiques of various representative schemes. A different, more regionally oriented solution was also proposed. This was premised on something like a mutual hostage theory. The interests of Muslims in Hindu majority provinces would be safeguarded by the fact that there would be a Hindu minority in Muslim majority provinces. But the question then arose: what about the Centre? If Muslims did not have something close to parity or some veto power at the Centre, would not the Centre be partial to Hindus? But if such provisions were made for Muslims, some cried back, won't that violate some principle of equality, giving Muslims special status in excess of numbers? Why should they get parity at the Centre? And so the argument went back and forth. Whatever one may think of the history of Hindu–Muslim relations, the almost sixty [seventy] years of negotiations did not produce a single representative scheme that was internally stable and fair, that did not run the risk of leaning in one direction or the other. Meanwhile the aspiration had been unleashed that the state that succeeds the empire be representative. But who shall it represent? 'All Indians' would be an obvious answer. But that answer would not solve the problem: how would the identities that differentiate Indians be represented, at least along this axis? Partition was a non-solution, but a non-solution to a problem that had proven insoluble. That it resulted in the context of an empire of long duration, and on the back of a nationalist movement as liberal and progressive as they come, does not augur well for similar problems elsewhere. Alfred Cobban's pithy formulation: India could neither be united nor divided.

But the crucial lesson from this is that once the problem was articulated as trying to find the terms of cooperation between two communities, there was never going to be a solution—one compatible with modern requirements of citizenship.

The debate over Partition is often pitched as one between advocates of partition and advocates of unity. But this is too simple. The key intellectual division is not between those who wanted a united territory and those who did not; the key distinction is between those who wanted a conception of citizenship beyond compulsory identities and those who did not. Many, who wanted a united India like Azad and Gandhi, nevertheless thought that India was indeed a collection of distinct communities, who could flourish together; Nehru and Ambedkar wanted to transcend that India. Azad and Iqbal may have different implications for the territorial unity of India, but their metaphysics of community identity is more similar. Azad's plea for unity is premised on segmented toleration, differentiated citizenship. An intellectually underrated figure these days, like Lala Lajpat Rai, for example, is actually closer to Nehru and Ambedkar in the way he thinks about finding a conception of citizenship transcending community than his politics would suggest.

The compromises of practical politics and opportunism blurred these intellectual lines and created strange bedfellows. This is a heretical thought. But in terms of underlying positions, in any other world, Nehru, Lajpat Rai, Ranade, Syama Prasad

Mookerjee, Ambedkar, perhaps even Jinnah would have been in a similar party: looking for conceptions of citizenship that transcended traditional community affiliation and created space for individual freedom. They happened to disagree on whether you could do it in one diverse nation. Gandhi, Azad, Purshottamdas Tandon, Deen Dayal Upadhyaya, and perhaps Iqbal would have been in a similar camp, the modernist project as enacting community identities rather than transcending them.

The deep psychological challenge we have to overcome is not just the threat of majoritarianism. That threat is easy to identify, at least intellectually. The deeper challenge is that as long as the idea of majority and minority, understood in ethnic terms, remain deeply embedded in our legal and political fabric, and colonize the way we see each other at every step, the threat to freedom and the possibility of conflict will remain. We need to create a political culture that moves from the idea of India as a federation of constantly balancing communities, to a zone of freedom with equal opportunities for individuals.

I want to end with removing a couple of misapprehensions that moving away from thinking of India as a federation of communities raises. The first is this. The claim is not that communities and identities will not flourish; it is rather that they will flourish as a result of the free choices of individuals, not protection by the state. Second, moving to a zone of freedom does not rule out all forms of differentiated rights. But the function of these would be to honour freedom, not to preserve identity. This would have to meet that burden of justification.

Our view of India as a federation of communities has given us diversity, but also limited our toleration. In some ways, it has prepared the ground for increased intolerance by weighing everything on the axis of collective identity. As Nirmal Verma used to point out, majoritarianism is the natural outgrowth of a culture that fails to think beyond majority and minority. The Congress thought, it could run Muslim and Hindu nationalism together; majoritarian versions of the BJP simply got rid of the minority bit. But the ground for it was prepared by the deep, compulsive entrenchment of the idea that community identities are inescapable. So we crafted a tolerance founded on community identity, not on individual rights and citizenship. If we care about freedom all kinds of identities will flourish. If we insist on circumscribing identities, neither identities nor freedom will flourish. In the seventieth year of India's democracy it needs to become a beacon of freedom.

In Our Idea of Utopia

SUNITA NARAIN

Sunita Narain, a researcher and journalist, has been working on environmental issues for the past thirty years. She is currently the director general of Centre for Science and Environment (CSE) and editor of the fortnightly magazine, *Down To Earth*. Narain has worked extensively on climate change, with a particular interest in advocating for an ambitious and equitable global agreement. In 2016, *TIME* magazine listed her as one of the most influential people in the world.

It is clear, now and forever, that the threat of climate change is real; it is urgent and emissions already accumulated in the atmosphere are changing our weather in dangerous and catastrophic ways. In India today, we can see the impacts of a changing climate. Already our monsoons are getting more variable, less predictable and very extreme. So when it rains, it pours—leaving farmers desperate after the storm, coping with destroyed crops, floods and then months of water scarcity. The poor in India are victims of climate change. They are the human face of a global tragedy.

It is not just India. Our interconnected and globalized world is hurtling towards two catastrophes, one caused by our need for economic growth, and the other by unparalleled and gluttonous consumption that releases emissions into the atmosphere. These greenhouse gas emissions, primarily emitted because we need energy, contain portents of a future being placed at great risk.

We have to then confront some tough points. One, environmental issues cannot be ignored if we want to secure life and health. Two, development has to take a different path, for we must—starting now—mitigate its visibly adverse impact. Three, since we live on a planet where warming has been unleashed, unbridled, what we do must be done at an extraordinary speed.

This is where we are today. We have Donald Trump, who openly denied climate change and still won the elections. A large majority stands with him. Calls for protectionism are growing in this already rich world. The UK's Brexit vote is also a testimony to this anger. It is the revenge of the rich, who did not get richer. It is the revenge of the educated; the well-off who believe they are entitled to more and that this is being taken away from them by the 'others'. This is also a time when the already developed world, which has long exhausted its quota of the global atmospheric space, wants to burn more fossil fuel for its growth. It believes it is growth deprived.

These are signs of economic growth going horribly wrong. Inequality and divisions between people are increasing. The same economic growth is also having a huge and devastating impact on the environment—the fallout has resulted in the growing toxicity in our air, water, land and food, and, of course, the ultimate cost of a changing climate. So, it is time we took stock of this model of growth led by unbridled consumerism. Forget the poor, it is not even working for the rich.

In India, we have bigger challenges. Our local environment is threatened—air is foul, rivers are dying and cities are drowning in their own garbage. All this is showing up in terms of our health. And this when we do not have the resources to first pollute and then clean up.

We have to do something when the global economy sputters and slows. This means our growth cannot be equated with becoming a factory for the richer world. The model of cheap labour and cheap goods that fuelled the last two decades of growth is over, even before Trump puts (or doesn't) the last nail in its coffin. We need to look for new pathways to prosperity and well-being.

In all this, there is yet another challenge of employment. Today's speed and scale of automation is much more than what we witnessed in the past, when machines first replaced humans on the factory floor. Now computing skills make work faster, more productive and pain-free. This means, on the one hand, our cheap labour is not as prized as before, and on the other hand, unemployment is going to grow exponentially. In a world that is already angry about the divisions in class and resentful of inequalities, this portends an even darker future. So, what is the way ahead?

When Thomas More wrote *Utopia*—the blueprint for an ideal society with no crime or poverty—he did not realize that human societies would work his ideas to death. We have to ask if utopia is not dystopia today.

For us, utopia translates into growth, without full stops. We believe that economic growth is a one-way street. If we continue on it without any stops, we will get everything. We will get rid of crime, because we will have funds to build armies to police the society. We will get rid of poverty because we will have money to trickle down. But in this growth-at-all-costs model, we do not contemplate that livelihoods of large numbers of people could be wiped out or marginalized. We do not contemplate the fact that the public institutions designed to protect and support the poor and voiceless would get eroded and destroyed by the new private institutions of the market.

So, in this world—our world—the poor have got poorer. But the rich have definitely got richer and the gap has increased. This in turn is leading to huge insecurities. We are no different. In today's India, this gap between the rich and poor is more evident and stark. It shows up in public discourse. It bends public policy.

But let's get back to what we never considered in our idea of utopia. We certainly never thought (and some even today do not think) that growth could become our 'climate cancer'. It could self-destruct.

Today, we are already witnessing the impact of the ever-changing weather and its disastrous effect on the livelihoods of the poor. In India we have devastating floods caused by extreme rain—a whole year's rain in one day. This destroys crops and takes lives. Then as farmers pick up the courage to replant, they are affected by freak hailstorms, cold waves, or something else that is not normal, taking away their crops once again. The freaky and the weird have become normal. This is not okay. This is not right. Also, remember that one flood or crippling drought takes away the development dividends for a long time. People have to pick up the threads and weave their lives once again.

Of course, it is not just climate change that is the cause of poverty in large parts of the world, including India. It is the ultimate flaw in our idea of utopia—that growth is all we need and it is for all. The fact is climate change is directly related to the model of economic growth as we know it today.

The fact also is that after years of negotiations over commas and full stops, the world is nowhere close to getting rid of its addiction to fossil fuels. Let's be clear about that. This is not only about India or China or all the late entrants to the Boys' Club of growth. It is about developed countries, simply because all of us want to be like them. These countries have not discarded their growth model that adds to emissions in the atmosphere and hence have long overused their share of the atmospheric commons.

So, what do we do? First and most importantly, we must recommit to the idea of India so that it can be built on the concept of justice, inclusive and equitable growth. We must do this not because of 'altruism' but because of necessity. We know today that we cannot have sustainable growth if growth is not affordable and inclusive.

Air Pollution in Our Cities

This is a public health nightmare. And this is the situation when only a minuscule number of people in Delhi and other cities in India drive a car. In Delhi, the estimate is that only 15 per cent commute by car. But air pollution is high and congestion is crippling. Can these cities combat air pollution, given that more and more people will opt for driving in the future? Is it possible to plan for the remaining 80–85 per cent? Is there space on the road, or space in the air?

Clearly, it is not possible. Our research has pointed out that unless we reinvent mobility at a scale not seen before, we cannot have clean air. A few years ago, in a landmark judgment, the

Delhi High Court ruled that roads need to be planned taking into account 'equity of use'—those who use more, should get more space. Today, the bulk of our cities' population walks, cycles or takes a bus. It does so because it is poor. But we need to take the bus, cycle or walk even if we are rich, and not wait till cars have occupied all the roads.

Therefore, unless the strategy to combat air pollution moves from fixing tailpipe emissions of each car to planning for affordable and inclusive mobility, we will not get clean air. This will not be easy. But one thing is clear—the solutions must work for the poor, for them to work for the rich.

Mosquitoes That Make People Sick

The fact is that mosquitoes do not distinguish between the rich and the poor. The fact also is that mosquitoes do not travel, people do. So, unless we clean our cities for all, diseases such as dengue and chikungunya will continue to take a deadly toll, and climate change will only make it worse. In today's India people fight high, even haemorrhagic, fever, excruciating joint pain and acute fatigue because of vector-borne diseases. The mortality rate is high, but what is worse, much worse, is morbidity and the illness-related disability that forces people out of jobs and regular activities for days together. Remember, this is even worse for daily wagers and our cities have millions of them. They cannot even take a day off; there is no sick leave available to them. These viral diseases, spread through mosquitoes, are debilitating. So, let's be clear—we are sick in our cities.

This, simply put, is the result of garbage, dirt, filth and neglect that surrounds us in urban India. It is also a fact that dengue and chikungunya are urban diseases. Studies have shown that prevalence of Aedes aegypti is much higher in urban areas as compared to rural areas. This mosquito has adapted to urban areas by moving from natural to artificial breeding habitats. An Aedes aegypti mosquito can breed inside an abandoned tyre or even a bottle cap with a little water.

It can also spread the virus fast in urban areas. This is not because the mosquito moves over a large area. In fact, the range of the mosquito is only 100 metres. What moves is the person bitten by the mosquito and infected by the virus. That person then transmits the virus to another mosquito, bred at another place, when it bites him or her. And in urban areas human density is high and so is the rate of transmission. This is the revenge of the mosquito. This much is clear. It is also clear that climate change makes for ideal conditions for more mosquitoes to breed—variable rain and then intense heat is a perfect breeding environment.

The only way out is to stop the breeding of mosquitoes. To do this, all the conditions conducive to its breeding need to be removed. In cities, this means cleaning up big time. There is no other option. It is also clear that we have allowed filth to grow in our vicinity for too long. This is because there don't seem to be any immediate or apparent repercussions. It looks bad, yes. But we have learnt to live with it. Even today, we are not able to comprehend the fact that mosquitoes do not move far and wide, humans do. Disease transmission requires mosquitoes as carriers, so mosquitoes have to be our target and obsessive cleaning up our only objective.

Dengue and chikungunya are urban India's nightmare. They will haunt us. They will make us sick. So clean up, obsessively.

The Crippling Drought

This results from our mismanagement of water which becomes scarcer in times of variable rain. The recent droughts in India have been different. In the 1990s, drought affected the poor India. But now it affects the richer and more water-guzzling India. This classless drought makes for a crisis that is more severe and solutions more complex.

In fact, the British-made drought code is outdated in today's India. Water demand has increased manifold. Today, people in cities have to drag water from miles away for their consumption. Industries, including power plants, take what they can from where they can. The water they use is returned as sewage or waste water. Then farmers grow commercial crops— from sugar cane to banana. They dig deeper and deeper into the ground to pump water for their irrigation needs. They have no way of telling when it will reach the point of no return. They only know this when the tube well goes dry.

This modern-day drought of water, which also affects the rich India, has to be combined with another development: climate change. The fact is that rain is become even more variable, unseasonal and extreme. In the future, this will only exacerbate the crisis. It is time we understood that drought is man-made and can be reversed. It can be managed. But then we really need to get our act together.

What needs to be done is as follows: First, do everything we can to augment our water resources—catch every drop of water, store it, recharge groundwater. To do this we need to build millions of structures, but this time based on planning for water and not just employment. This means the plan has to be deliberate and purposeful. It also means giving people the right to decide where they want the waterbody to be located and the right to manage it for their need. Today, invariably, the land on which the waterbody is built belongs to one department, and the land from where the water is harvested and the channels from where the water is brought belong to a second or even a third government department. There is no synergy in this system. No water is harvested. The employment that is provided during one drought should be used to build security against the next one.

We must also obsessively work to save water at all times. This means insisting on water codes for everyday India. We need to reduce water usage in all the sectors—from agriculture to urban to industry. This means benchmarking the use and setting targets for reduced consumption year-on-year. It means doing everything from introducing water-efficient fixtures to promoting crops that consume less water. It means making our war against drought permanent. Only then will drought not become permanent.

Water Pollution

Indian rivers are becoming increasingly polluted, but again the question is whether we can clean them when a large number of people do not have access to sanitation and clean water.

A 2012 Centre for Science and Environment (CSE) report, *Excreta Matters,* showed why policy had to change. The current system of water and waste management is capital-intensive and it creates division between the rich and the poor.

The state has limited resources and can only invest in providing for some—invariably the rich and not the poor. But if only a part of the city has access to clean water and underground sewerage, pollution control will not work. The reason is simple: the treated waste of a few will be mixed with the untreated waste of many. The end result is and always will be pollution.

It is also clear that the greater the pollution, the higher the cost of cleaning the water. Even the rich in our cities cannot afford the current costs of delivering water, then taking back waste and treating it before disposing it into rivers. So, either water is not supplied to all or sewage is not treated. The solution has to be to invest in affordable solutions for water and waste that meet the needs of all. Only then can we clean our rivers.

Climate Change

In 1990, my colleague Anil Agarwal and I argued in our publication, *Global Warming in an Unequal World,* that the world cannot combat climate change unless the agreement is fair and equitable. Today, the same issue is on the table. If the solutions cannot meet the needs of all—are equitable—they will not work. The global carbon budget—the amount of carbon dioxide that can be emitted without crossing the threshold of temperature rise—has been disproportionately appropriated by the rich. Their current lack of aspiration for change means they continue to emit more, thus take up more space. But one should understand that economic growth is linked to emissions; so tomorrow the poor, who are getting richer, will also pollute. In this way, all will be at risk.

The solution is not to ask the poor not to get rich. This is what the Paris Agreement on climate change, signed last December, is hoping to get away with. It is built on the premise that the last part of the still-developing world can build its future on a limited and minimal share of the global carbon budget. It assumes that the world does not need to emit to grow, or not need to grow at all. This is not possible. So, what will happen is that India and many in Africa will add to the carbon dioxide in the atmosphere. This will mean that the world will not be able to keep the temperature rise below the safe threshold. *Climate justice is not a luxury, but a prerequisite for an effective deal.*

It is then clear that the discourse on our idea of India and utopia must be reframed so that it is built on the premise that sustainable development is not possible if it is not equitable. In other words, growth has to be affordable and inclusive.

But most important is that we rearticulate the fact that the environmental challenge is not technocratic but political. We cannot neuter politics of access, justice and rights, and still hope to fix environmental problems or get the right to development.

But most of all, we must fix development for the poorest in the country, those who are and will be worst affected by climate change. Our farmers are already caught in a spiral of debt because of the increasing cost of agriculture and now extreme and variable weather is the last straw.

Meteorologists will tell you that the weather is becoming more erratic, more confounding and definitely more devastating.

Monsoon is our finance minister and it is not just capricious, but perhaps the most globalized Indian. We need to invest in the science of monsoons and weather forecasting.

Then, we need to do much more to fix our agrarian crisis. It is clear that farmers are caught in a double bind. On the one hand, costs of all inputs, particularly labour and water, are increasing, and on the other hand, there are controls on food prices. Our food pricing policy is built on the premise that we are a poor country, so consumers must be protected. But this means farmers—who are also consumers of food—are not paid remunerative prices for their product. And all the big talk about deregulation and ease of doing business never makes it to their fields. There are restrictions on where they can sell; prices are artificially 'fixed'; and when shortages grow, the government rushes to buy from heavily subsidized global farms. This cannot go on.

We need to plan for development, knowing that the weather will be more variable and more extreme. This means doing all that we know has to be done. There is no rocket science here. Build water and drainage infrastructure that can both hold water when there is excess rain and recharge groundwater when it is scarce. We are not even using the optimal potential of rural employment to build water security.

We have just not understood that in a climate-risked India, water has to be our main focus. Infrastructure—everything from cities and roads to ports and dams—must be built in a way that they are compliant with the best environmental safeguards.

Also, knowing that building resilience and adapting to these changes is not enough, we need to vastly strengthen systems to compute farmers' losses and pay for damage—quickly and properly. At present, our so-called crop insurance schemes are poorly designed and even more poorly executed. Once again, this cannot go on.

Let's get our heads out of the sand and smell the wind. Only then can we stop the killing fields.

Intolerance Must Go

There is another change we must bring about so that utopia does not turn into dystopia. We must change the idea that we are a tolerant society, because we are actually a civil society.

In December 2016, at the Paris climate conference, when the debate on intolerance was at its height in India, there was another side to intolerance that I could see. Intolerance towards climate change meant that for the first time, since the beginning of climate negotiations, the erstwhile climate renegades were in control of the dialogue, the narrative and the audience.

The Umbrella Group is a grouping led by the US and includes the biggest rich polluters, such as Australia and Japan, who have always been in the dock for not taking action to combat climate change. In Paris, these countries went through an unbelievable image makeover.

This was done by systematically and systemically decimating any counter-voices or differing opinions. So, for instance, when the Indian delegation (meekly) asked for the climate agreement to be both effective and equitable—taking into account past contributions to the greenhouse problem—they were scolded or simply ignored.

What Western governments could not do, their media did with great aplomb. The *New York Times*, for instance, was quick to publish a cartoon terming India as the roadblock to a successful climate deal—an elephant blocking the railroad—and significantly said that this would end up destroying then US President Barack Obama's legacy.

So, intolerance was scripted so that the other side's version could be erased. In this way, the Paris climate change talk ended with an agreement which was far from ambitious and a long way from being equitable.

The global Paris Agreement on climate change tells us, more than ever, that the world has bubble-wrapped itself, and believes that nobody can prick it or burst through. To be secure in the bubble, conversation is restricted to only what is convenient. In this age of Internet-enabled information, ironically, we are actually reading and being sensitive to less, not more. The circles of information have shrunk to what is most agreeable to listen to. It is no surprise, then, that in climate change negotiations—in trade talks or international relations—there is one dominant discourse.

We need to ask why there should be such a breakdown in communication in such well-informed, literate societies and in times when everybody is so well connected to the Internet and social media.

We have become an increasingly less informed society as our circles of information have shrunk. This means we are also a divided and disconnected society as we have no understanding of the other's position. The trend continues on social media. We follow people whose opinion we value. When we say anything that is unpalatable to the other side, we get trolled. We then engage even less. The door closes.

Institutions for Whom?

This is what is leading to our fatal refusal to fathom, or approach, opinions or realities that are different. The growing inequality in the world is also part of this inability to see the counter-view of utopia. In this utopian world no amount of growth and economic prosperity is enough any more, because aspiration is the new god. This means that anybody who is poor is marginalized simply because they have just not made the grade. There is no longer space for such 'failure' in our braver, newer world.

It is important to rethink the question of states, market and society. We have dismembered the state; grown the market; and believed that we have empowered the society. We believed that people would be modulating voices over the market. They were the safeguards.

But we forgot to ask—which society is being empowered and for what? And so slowly, the circles closed—the state market and the aspiring consuming society merged. Became one. Anyone outside this circle was not counted. They were slowly erased. Think about it. In this state-market-society world, it is about the survival of the fittest, in a way that would have made Darwin insane.

So, in the coming years, we have to insistently ask—which society are we talking about. The poor or the rich? So, this is also a part of the development challenge—deepening and strengthening democracy, not just for the socially connected but for all.

So it is time we rewrote our own *Utopia*; we re-envisioned our future directions of growth so that it is inclusive and sustainable. And all this can only happen when cultures embrace tolerance like never before. These are not words but imperatives. Essentials. Prerequisites for our secure future. This is what utopia—the idea of India—means in a climate-risked world.

The Idea of an Ever-ever Land

SHASHI THAROOR

Shashi Tharoor, an author, politician and former international civil servant, is a second-term Lok Sabha member, representing Thiruvananthapuram, and the chairman of the parliamentary standing committee on external affairs. During his nearly three-decade-long career at the United Nations, he served as a peacekeeper, refugee worker and an administrator. Tharoor is also the author of sixteen books, both fiction and non-fiction.

At midnight on 15 August 1947, independent India was born as its first prime minister, Jawaharlal Nehru, proclaimed 'a tryst with destiny—a moment which comes but rarely in history, when we pass from the old to the new, when an age ends and when the soul of a nation, long suppressed, finds utterance'. With those words he launched India on a remarkable experiment in governance. Remarkable because it was happening at all. 'India,' Winston Churchill once barked, 'is merely a geographical expression. It is no more a single country than the equator.' Churchill was rarely right about India, but it is true that no other country in the world embraces the extraordinary mixture of ethnic groups, the profusion of mutually incomprehensible languages, the varieties of topography and climate, the diversity of religions and cultural practices and the range of levels of economic development like India does.

And yet India, I have long argued, is more than the sum of its contradictions. It is a country held together, in the words of Nehru, 'by strong but invisible threads . . . a myth and an idea, a dream and a vision, and yet very real and present and pervasive'.

Just thinking about India makes clear the immensity of the challenge of defining what the idea of India means. How does one approach this land of snow peaks and tropical jungles, with twenty-three major languages and 22,000 distinct 'dialects' (including some spoken by more people than Danish or Norwegian), inhabited in the second decade of the twenty-first century by over a billion individuals of every ethnic extraction known to humanity? How does one come to terms with a country whose population is nearly 30 per cent illiterate but which has educated the world's second-largest pool of trained scientists and engineers, whose teeming cities overflow while two out of three Indians scratch a living from the soil? What is the clue to understanding a country rife with despair and disrepair, which nonetheless moved a Mughal emperor to declaim, 'if on earth there be paradise of bliss, it is this, it is this, it is this . . .'? How does one gauge a culture which elevated non-violence to an effective moral principle, but whose freedom was born in blood and whose independence still soaks in it? How does one explain a land where peasant organizations and suspicious officials once attempted to close down Kentucky Fried Chicken as a threat to the nation, where a former prime minister once bitterly criticized the sale of Pepsi-Cola 'in a country where villagers don't have clean drinking water', and which yet invents more sophisticated software for the planet's computer manufacturers than any other country in the world? How can one determine the future of an ageless civilization that was the birthplace of four major religions, a dozen different traditions of classical dance, eighty-five major political parties and 300 ways of cooking potato?

The short answer is that it can't be done, at least not to everyone's satisfaction. Any truism about India can be immediately contradicted by another truism about India. It is often jokingly said that 'anything you can say about India, the opposite is also true'. The country's national motto, emblazoned on its governmental crest, is 'Satyameva Jayate': Truth Alone Triumphs. The question remains, however, whose truth? It is a question to which there are at least a billion answers, if the last census hasn't undercounted us again.

But that sort of an answer is no answer at all, and so another answer to those questions has to be sought. And this may lie in a simple insight: the singular thing about India is that you can only speak of it in the plural. There are, in the hackneyed phrase, many Indias. Everything exists in countless variants. There is no single standard, no fixed stereotype, no 'one way'. This pluralism is acknowledged in the way India arranges its own affairs: all groups, faiths, tastes and ideologies survive and contend for their place in the sun. At a time when most developing countries opted for authoritarian models of government to promote nation building and to direct development, India chose to be a multiparty democracy. And despite many stresses and strains, including twenty-two months of autocratic rule during the 1975 Emergency, a multiparty democracy—freewheeling, rumbustious, corrupt and inefficient, perhaps, but nonetheless flourishing—India has remained.

One result is that India strikes many as maddening, chaotic, inefficient and seemingly 'unpurposeful' as it muddles its way through the second decade of the twenty-first century. Another, though, is that India is not just a country, it is an adventure, one in which all avenues are open and everything is possible. 'India,' wrote the British historian E.P. Thompson, 'is perhaps the most important country for the future of the world. All the convergent influences of the world run through this society . . . There is not a thought that is being thought in the West or East that is not active in some Indian mind.'

Just as well a Brit said that, and not an Indian! That Indian mind has been shaped by remarkably diverse forces: ancient Hindu tradition, myth and scripture; the impact of Islam and Christianity; and two centuries of British colonial rule. The result is unique. Many observers have been astonished by India's survival as a pluralist state. But India could hardly have survived as anything else. Pluralism is a reality that emerges from the very nature of the country; it is a choice made inevitable by India's geography and reaffirmed by its history.

Pluralism and inclusiveness have long marked the idea of India. India's is a civilization that, over millennia, has offered refuge and, more importantly, religious and cultural freedom to Jews, Parsis, several varieties of Christians and, of course, Muslims. Jews came to Kerala centuries before Christ, with the destruction of their First Temple by the Babylonians, and they knew no persecution on Indian soil until the Portuguese arrived in the sixteenth century to inflict it. Christianity arrived on Indian soil with St Thomas the Apostle (Doubting Thomas), who came to the Kerala coast some time before 52 CE and was welcomed on shore by a flute-playing Jewish girl. He made many converts, so there are Indians today whose ancestors were Christian well before any Europeans discovered Christianity. In Kerala, where Islam came through traders, travellers and missionaries rather than by the sword, the Zamorin of Calicut was so impressed by the seafaring skills of this community that he issued a decree obliging each fisherman's family to bring up one son as a Muslim to man his all-Muslim navy! This is India, a land whose heritage of diversity means that in the Kolkata neighbourhood where I lived during my high school years, the wail of the muezzin calling the Islamic faithful to prayer routinely blends with the chant of mantras and the tinkling of bells at the local Shiva temple, accompanied by the Sikh gurdwara's reading of verses from the Guru Granth Sahib, with St Paul's cathedral just round the corner.

So the first challenge is that we cannot generalize about India. One of the few generalizations that can safely be made about India is that nothing can be taken for granted about the country. Not even its name: for the word India comes from the river Indus, which flows in Pakistan. That anomaly is easily explained, for we know that Pakistan was hacked off the stooped shoulders of India by the departing British in 1947. (Yet each explanation breeds another anomaly. Pakistan was created as a homeland for India's Muslims, but—at least till very recently—there were more Muslims in India than in Pakistan.)

How, then, does one define the Indian idea?

This nebulous 'idea of India'—though the phrase is Tagore's—is, in some form or another, arguably as old as antiquity itself. However, the idea of India as a modern nation based on a certain conception of human rights and citizenship, vigorously backed by due process of law and equality before law, is relatively recent.

The British like to point out, in moments of self-justifying exculpation, that it's their achievement; that they deserve credit for the political unity of India—indeed, that the very idea of 'India' as one entity (now three, but one during the British Raj) instead of multiple warring principalities and statelets is the unchallengeable contribution of the British imperial rule. I have gone at length into this claim in my recent book *An Era of Darkness* (2016).

As I point out, it is difficult to refute that proposition except with a provable hypothesis: that throughout the history of the subcontinent, there has existed an impulsion for unity. This was manifest in the several kingdoms throughout Indian history that sought to extend their reach across all of the subcontinent: the Maurya (322 BCE–185 BCE), Gupta (at its peak, 320–550 CE) and Mughal (1526–1857 CE) empires, and, to a lesser extent, the Vijayanagara Kingdom in the Deccan (at its peak, 1136–1565 CE) and the Maratha confederacy (1674–1818 CE). Every period of disorder throughout Indian history has been followed by a centralizing impulse, and had the British not been the first to take advantage of India's disorder with superior weaponry, it is entirely possible that an Indian ruler would have accomplished what the British did, and consolidated his rule over most of the subcontinent.

The same impulse is also manifest in Indians' vision of our own nation, as in the ancient epics the Mahabharata and the Ramayana, which reflect an 'idea of India' that twentieth-century nationalists would have recognized. The epics have acted as strong, yet sophisticated, threads of Indian culture that have woven together tribes, languages and peoples across the subcontinent, uniting them in their celebration of the same larger-than-life heroes and heroines, whose stories were told in dozens of translations and variations but always in the same spirit and meaning. The landscape the Pandavas saw in the Mahabharata (composed approximately in the period 400 BCE to 400 CE) was a pan-Indian landscape, for instance, as their travels throughout it demonstrated, and through their tale, Indians speaking hundreds of languages and thousands of dialects in all the places named in the epic, enjoying a civilizational unity. Lord Rama's journey through India and his epic battle against the demon-king of Lanka reflect the same national idea.

After all, India has enjoyed cultural and geographical unity throughout the ages, going back at least to Emperor Ashoka in the third century BCE. The vision of Indian unity was physically embodied by the Hindu sage Adi Shankara, who travelled from Kerala in the extreme south to Kashmir in the extreme north and from Dwarka in the west to Puri in the east, as far back as the seventh century after Christ, establishing temples in each of these places that endure to this day. Diana Eck's writings on India's 'sacred geography' extensively delineate ancient ideas of a political unity mediated through ideas of sacredness. As Eck explains, 'Considering its long history, India has had but a few hours of political and administrative unity. Its unity as a nation, however, has been firmly constituted by the sacred geography it has held in common and revered: its mountains, forests, rivers, hilltop shrines . . . linked with the tracks of pilgrimage.'

Nor was this oneness a purely 'Hindu' idea. The rest of the world saw India as one: Arabs, for instance, regarded the entire subcontinent as 'al-Hind' and all Indians as 'Hindi', whether they hailed from Punjab, Bengal or Kerala. The great nationalist Maulana Azad once remarked upon how, at the Haj, all Indians were considered by other Muslims to be from one land—all 'Hindis'—and regarded themselves as such. Surely such impulses, fulfilled in those distant times by emperors and sages, would with modern transport, communications and far-sighted leaders have translated themselves into political unity?

Counterfactuals are, of course, impossible to prove. One cannot assert, for instance, with any degree of certitude, events that did not in fact occur, nor name that centralizing figure who might have been India's Bismarck, Mazzini, Atatürk or Garibaldi in the absence of the British. But historical events find their own dramatis personae, and it is unreasonable to suggest that what happened everywhere else would not have happened in India. Counterfactuals are theoretical, but facts are what they are. The facts point clearly to the dismantling of the preexisting political institutions of India by the British, the fomenting of communal division and systematic political discrimination with a view to maintain and extend British domination.

In the years after their victory at the Battle of Plassey, in 1757, the British astutely fomented cleavages among the Indian princes, and steadily consolidated their dominion through a policy of 'divide and rule' that came to be dubbed, after 1858, *'divide et impera'*. The sight of Hindu and Muslim soldiers rebelling together in 1857 and fighting side by side, willing to rally under the command of each other and pledge joint allegiance to the enfeebled Mughal monarch, alarmed the British, who did not take long to conclude that dividing the two groups and pitting them against one another was the most effective way to ensure the unchallenged continuance of the Empire. As early as 1859, the then British governor of Bombay, Lord Elphinstone, advised London that '*Divide et impera* was the old Roman maxim, and it should be ours'. The creation and perpetuation of Hindu–Muslim antagonism was the most significant accomplishment of the British imperial policy: the project of *divide et impera* would reach its culmination in the horrors of Partition that eventually accompanied the collapse of the British authority in 1947. It is difficult, therefore, to buy the self-serving imperial argument that Britain bequeathed to India its political unity and democracy.

I would argue, as Nehru did, that the idea of India has always been inherent in our civilization. This is why, when Jinnah argued that religion was a valid determinant of nationhood, and demanded a separate country for India's Muslims, Nehru never accepted his logic. To do so would have been to reduce India to a country of and for Hindus, and this, Nehru saw, would do violence to the idea of India that he cherished, valued so greatly and articulated so powerfully.

Earlier conceptions of India drew their inspiration from mythology and theology. However, the modern idea of India, despite the mystical influence of Tagore and the spiritual and moral influences of Gandhiji, is a robustly secular and legal construct based upon the vision and intellect of our founding fathers, notably (in alphabetical order) Ambedkar, Nehru and Patel. The preamble of the Constitution itself is the most eloquent enumeration of this vision. In its description of the defining traits of the Indian republic, in its conception of justice, of liberty, of equality and fraternity, it firmly proclaims that the law will be the bedrock of the idea of India.

How did India preserve and protect a viable idea of itself in the course of the last sixty-nine years, while it grew from 370 million people to 1.3 billion, reorganized its state structures and sought to defend itself from internal and external dangers, all the while remaining democratic? I have tried to answer this question at length in my books. Certainly the accomplishment is extraordinary and worthy of celebration. Amid India's myriad problems, it is democracy that has given Indians of every imaginable caste, creed, culture and cause the chance to break free of their age-old subsistence-level existence.

There is social oppression and caste tyranny, particularly in rural India, but Indian democracy offers the victims a means of escape, and often—thanks to the determination with which the poor and oppressed exercise their franchise—of triumph. The various schemes established by the UPA government for the betterment of the rural poor are a result of this connection between our citizens and the state.

And yet, in the nearly seven decades since Independence, democracy has failed to create a single political community. Instead, we have become more conscious than ever of what divides us: religion, region, caste, language, ethnicity. The political system has become looser and more fragmented. Politicians mobilize support along ever-narrower lines of political identity. It has become more important to be a 'backward caste', a 'tribal', or a religious sectarian than to be an Indian; and of course, to some it is more important to be a 'proud' Hindu than to be an Indian. This is particularly ironic because one of the early strengths of Nehruvian India—the survival of the nationalist movement as a political party, the Congress Party serving as an all-embracing, all-inclusive agglomeration of the major political tendencies in the country—stifled the normal process of contention over political principle. With the emergence and growth of other political forces, politicians have been tempted to organize themselves around identities other than parties (or to create parties to reflect a specific identity).

Caste, which Nehru and his ilk abhorred and believed would disappear from the social matrix of modern India, has not merely survived and thrived but has become an instrument for highly effective political mobilization. Candidates are picked by their parties with an eye towards the caste loyalties they can call upon; often their appeal is overtly to voters of their own caste or sub-caste, urging them to elect one of their own. The result has been the growth of caste consciousness and casteism throughout the society. In many states, caste determines educational opportunities, job prospects and governmental promotions; all too often, people say you cannot go forward unless you're a 'backward'.

Ironically, a distinctive feature of the Nehruvian legacy was its visionary rejection of India's assorted bigotries and particularisms. All four generations of Nehrus in public life remained secular in outlook and conduct. Their appeal transcended caste, region, language and religion, something virtually impossible to say of most other leading Indian politicians.

Whether through elections or quotas, political mobilization in contemporary India has asserted the power of old identities, habits, faiths and prejudices. Transcending them will be a major challenge for the Indian polity in the twenty-first century.

One does question: What makes India a nation? In a country notorious for identity politics, especially at election time, we may well ask: What is an Indian's identity?

When an Italian nation was created in the second half of the nineteenth century out of a mosaic of principalities and small states, one Italian nationalist, Massimo Taparelli d'Azeglio, wrote, 'We have created Italy. Now all we need to do is to create Italians.'

It is striking that, half a century later, no Indian nationalist succumbed to the temptation to express a similar thought. The prime exponent of modern Indian nationalism, Nehru, would have never spoken of 'creating Indians', because he believed that India and Indians had existed for millennia before he articulated their political aspirations in the twentieth century.

Nonetheless, the India that was born in 1947 was in a very real sense a new creation: a state that made fellow citizens of the Ladakhi and the Laccadivian, divided Punjabi from Punjabi and asked a Keralite peasant to feel allegiance to a Kashmiri Pandit ruling in Delhi, all for the first time.

Let me illustrate what this means with a simple story. When India celebrated the forty-ninth anniversary of its independence from British rule fifteen years ago, our then prime minister, H.D. Deve Gowda, stood at the ramparts of Delhi's seventeenth-century Red Fort and delivered the traditional Independence Day address to the nation in Hindi, India's 'national language'. Eight other prime ministers had done exactly the same thing forty-eight times before him, but what was unusual this time was that Deve Gowda, a southerner from the state of Karnataka, spoke to the country in a language of which he did not know a word. Tradition and politics required a speech in Hindi, so he gave one—the words having been written out for him in his native Kannada script, in which they, of course, made no sense.

Such an episode is almost inconceivable elsewhere, but it represents the best of the oddities that help make India. Only in India could a country be ruled by a man who does not understand its 'national language'; only in India, for that matter, is there a 'national language' which half the population does not understand; and only in India could this particular solution be found to enable the prime minister to address his people. One of Indian cinema's finest 'playback singers', the Keralite K.J. Yesudas, sang his way to the top of the Hindi music charts with lyrics in that language written in the Malayalam script for him, but to see the same practice elevated to the prime ministerial address on Independence Day was a startling affirmation of Indian pluralism.

For, you see, we are all minorities in India. A typical Indian stepping off a train, a Hindi-speaking Hindu male from the Gangetic plain state of Uttar Pradesh, might cherish the illusion that he represents the 'majority community', to use an expression much favoured by the less industrious of our journalists. But he does not. As a Hindu he belongs to the faith adhered to by some 81 per cent of the population, but a majority of the country does not speak Hindi; a majority does not hail from Uttar Pradesh; and if he were visiting, say, Kerala, he would discover that a majority there is not even male. Worse, our archetypal UP Hindu has only to mingle with the polyglot, multicoloured crowds (and I'm referring to the colour of their skins, not their clothes) thronging any of India's major railway stations to realize how much of a minority he really is. Even his Hinduism is no guarantee of 'majorityhood', because his caste automatically places him in a minority as well: if he is a Brahmin, 90 per cent of his fellow Indians are not; if he is a Yadav, a 'backward class', 85 per cent of Indians are not, and so on.

Or take language. The Constitution of India recognizes twenty-three today—our demonetized rupee notes give the denomination in fourteen scripts—but in fact, there are thirty-five Indian languages which are spoken by more than a million people; and these languages have their own scripts, grammatical structures and cultural assumptions, not just dialects (and if we were to count dialects within these languages, there are more than 22,000). Each of the native speakers of these languages is in a linguistic minority, for none enjoys the majority status in India. Thanks in part to the popularity of Mumbai's Hindi cinema, Hindi is understood, if not always well spoken, by nearly half the population of India, but it is in no sense the language of the majority; indeed, its locutions, gender rules and script are unfamiliar to most Indians in the south or north-east.

Ethnicity further complicates the notion of a majority community. Most of the time, an Indian's name immediately reveals where he is from and what his mother tongue is; when we introduce ourselves we are advertising our origins. Despite some intermarriages at the elite levels in the cities, Indians still largely remain endogamous, and a Bengali is easily distinguished from a Punjabi. The difference this reflects is often more apparent than the elements of commonality. A Karnataka Brahmin shares his Hindu faith with a Bihari Kurmi, but feels little identity with him in respect of appearance, dress, customs, tastes, language or political objectives. At the same time a Tamil Hindu would feel that he has far more in common with a Tamil Christian or Muslim than with, say, a Haryanvi Jat with whom he formally shares a religion.

Why do I harp on these differences? Only to make the point that Indian nationalism is a rare animal indeed. This land imposes no narrow conformities on its citizens: you can be many things and one thing. You can be a good Muslim, a good Keralite and a good Indian all at once. When Yugoslavia was tearing itself apart in a civil war among peoples all descended from the same Slavic tribes that had settled the Balkan Peninsula a millennium earlier, learned Freudians pointed to the disagreements that arise out of 'the narcissism of minor differences'. But in India we celebrate the commonality of major differences. To stand Michael Ignatieff's famous phrase on its head, we are a land of belonging rather than of blood.

So Indian nationalism is not based on any of the conventional indices of national identity. Not language, since our constitution now recognizes twenty-three official languages, and as many as thirty-five languages spoken by more than a million people each.

Not ethnicity, since the 'Indian' accommodates a diversity of racial types in which many Indians (Punjabis and Bengalis, in particular) have more ethnically in common with foreigners (Pakistanis and Bangladeshis) than with their other compatriots (Poonawallas and Bangaloreans).

Not religion, since India is a secular pluralist state that is home to every religion known to mankind, with the possible exception of Shintoism.

Not geography, since the natural geography of the subcontinent—framed by the mountains and the sea—was hacked by the Partition of 1947.

And not even territory, since, by law, anyone with one grandparent born in pre-partition India—outside the territorial boundaries of today's state—is eligible for citizenship. Indian nationalism has therefore always been the nationalism of an idea.

It is the idea of an ever-ever land, emerging from an ancient civilization, united by a shared history, sustained by pluralist democracy. India's democracy imposes no narrow conformities on its citizens.

So the idea of India is of one land embracing many. Geography helps, because it accustoms Indians to the idea of difference.

The Indian idea, as I have long argued, is that a nation may endure differences of caste, creed, colour, conviction, culture, cuisine, costume and custom, and still rally around a consensus. And that consensus is around the simple idea that in a democracy you don't really need to agree, except on the ground rules of how you will disagree.

My generation grew up in an India where our sense of nationhood lay in the slogan, 'unity in diversity'. We were brought up to take pluralism for granted and to reject the communalism that had partitioned the nation when the British left. In rejecting the case for Pakistan, Indian nationalism also rejected the very idea that religion should be a determinant of nationhood. We never fell into the insidious trap of agreeing that, since Partition had established a state for Muslims, what remained was a state for Hindus. To accept the idea of India you had to spurn the logic that had divided the country.

This was what that much-abused term 'secularism' meant for us. Western dictionaries defined 'secularism' as the absence of religion, but Indian secularism meant a profusion of religions; the state engaged with all of them but privileged none. Secularism in India did not mean irreligiousness, which even avowedly atheist parties like the communists or the southern DMK party found unpopular amongst their voters; indeed, in Kolkata's annual Durga Puja, the communist parties compete with each other to put up the most lavish puja pandals, pavilions to the goddess Durga. Rather, secularism meant, in the Indian tradition, multireligiousness. The Kolkata neighbourhood I described earlier epitomized this India.

Throughout the decades after Independence, the political culture of the country reflected these 'secular' assumptions and attitudes. Though the Indian population is 81 per cent Hindu and the country had been partitioned as a result of a demand for a separate Muslim homeland, three of India's thirteen presidents have been Muslims; so were innumerable governors, cabinet ministers, chief ministers of states, ambassadors, generals and Supreme Court justices (and chief justices). During the war with Pakistan in 1971, the Indian Air Force in the northern sector was commanded by a Muslim (Lateef); the army commander was a Parsi (Manekshaw), the general officer commanding the forces that marched into Bangladesh was a Sikh (Aurora), and the general flown in to negotiate the surrender of the Pakistani forces in East Bengal was Jewish (Jacob). *That* is India.

Not all agree with this vision of India. There are those who wish it to become a Hindu Rashtra, a land of and for the Hindu majority; they have made gains in the elections of the 1990s and in the politics of the street. Secularism is established in India's Constitution, but they ask why India should not, like many other Third World countries, find refuge in the assertion of what they call its own religious identity. We have all seen the outcome of this view in the horrors that have cost perhaps 2000 lives in Gujarat a decade and a half ago.

Those riots, like the killing of the Sikhs in reaction to Indira Gandhi's assassination in 1984, were fundamentally violative of the idea of India. India has survived the Aryans, the Mughals, the British; it has taken from each—language, art, food, learning—and grown with all of them. To be Indian is to be part of an elusive dream we all share, a dream that fills our minds with sounds, words, flavours from many sources that we cannot easily identify. Large, eclectic, agglomerative, the Hinduism that I know understands that faith is a matter of hearts and minds, not of bricks and stone. 'Build Ram in your heart,' the Hindu is enjoined; and if Ram is in your heart, it will little matter where else he is, or is not.

Chauvinism and anti-minority violence has emerged from the competition for resources in a contentious democracy. Politicians of all faiths across India seek to mobilize voters by appealing to narrow identities; by seeking votes in the name of religion, caste and region, they have urged voters to define themselves on these lines. As religion, caste and region have come to dominate public discourse, to some it has become more important to be a Muslim, a Bodo or a Yadav than to be an Indian.

This is why the change in the public discourse about Indianness is so dangerous. The notion of majority and minority, as I have suggested, is fundamentally un-Indian and fails to reflect the real nature of our society. The suggestion that only a Hindu, and only a certain kind of Hindu, can be an authentic Indian is an affront to the very premise of Indian nationalism. An India that denies itself to some of us could end up being denied to all of us.

As the past is used by some to haunt the present, the cycle of violence goes on, spawning new hostages to history, ensuring that future generations will be taught new wrongs to set right. We live, Octavio Paz once wrote, between oblivion and memory. Memory and oblivion: how one leads to the other, and back again, has been the concern of much of my fiction. As I pointed out in the last words of my novel *Riot*, history is not a web woven with innocent hands.

The reduction of any group of Indians to second-class status in their homeland is unthinkable. It would be a second Partition: and a partition in the Indian soul would be as bad as a partition in the Indian soil.

My idea of India celebrates diversity: if America is a melting pot, as I have long argued, then to me India is a thali, a selection of sumptuous dishes in different bowls. Each tastes different, and does not necessarily mix with the next, but they belong together on the same plate and they complement each other in making the meal a satisfying repast.

This is the idea of India that we must defend at all costs. India's founding fathers wrote a constitution for their dreams; we have given passports to their ideals. Today these ideals are contested not only by stone-throwing young men in the streets of Srinagar and rifle-wielding Maoists in the forests of Chhattisgarh, but also by self-righteous triumphalists in the ruling party who proclaim that all Indians must subscribe to their narrow vision of Hindutva as an alternative to a more capacious Indianness.

They advocate a nationalism that is divisive rather than inclusive, embodied in a chauvinism intolerant of diversity and difference.

My idea of India gives me the right to chant 'Bharat mata ki jai'. It also gives me the right not to say it if I don't wish to. This is the right the custodians of today's nationalism would take away from me.

This is a battle for India's soul. All of us who believe in the liberal values embodied in our Constitution must strive to ensure that the ultimate winner must be the idea of India. Indians must remain faithful to our founding values of the twentieth century if we are to conquer the twenty-first.

An Indian Feminist at Seventy

ARUNA ROY

Aruna Roy, the founder member of Mazdoor Kisan Shakti Sangathan (MKSS), the National Campaign for People's Right to Information (NCPRI), and the School for Democracy, is a sociopolitical activist and a former IAS officer. She has worked for accessing constitutional rights for the poor, right to information, employment, food security, etc. She was listed as one of the 100 most influential people in the world by the *TIME* magazine in 2011.

When I was asked to write about women's struggles of the last seventy years, I assented without demur. But as I began to write, I was troubled by an India promoting inequality in religion, and discriminating in every possible way against its people, violating constitutional sanctity. It began intruding on a forty-year-old narrative. The discourse has a sexist and communal world view, and contradicts with disdain the tenets of a constitution we gave ourselves sixty-seven years ago. The assault is on equality and constitutional guarantees—be it secularism, right to freedom of expression, women's public and personal behaviour. Yet the people have gone to the polls and cast votes to 'democratically' elect their leaders. Any attempt India has made to set the balance right through guarantee of fundamental rights, reservations per se, has been mindlessly dismissed. But history cannot be set aside, nor empowerment sacrificed. This is a toast to those who fought collective battles against the most severe odds and won. We belong to that community.

There are more struggles ahead and victories too . . . I have journeyed with Naurti and Nandini to dialogue our way through this narrative. We look forward to newer and better stories . . .

Conversations with Two Contemporary Feminists on Activism and Change

Independent India is where inequality gets public sanction and religious identity takes over all else, and to try and present even a segment of seventy years of activism and feminism here is a daunting task. India is large and has been witness to thousands of struggles small and large, ranging from poor women who fought for the right to access food, to those who took on the might of the state, or even assumed formal positions of power. But essentially, it is the composition of the struggle that unites us: its principles and its complexities. Large numbers of Indian women would still seem absolutely untouched by many of these changes, and yet there is no doubt that the social, legal and constitutional framework has changed in fundamental ways. With it the potential position of all women in India has changed too.

In 1976, not long after I had resigned from the IAS and gone to live and work in rural Rajasthan, I got a letter from a wonderful woman named Jill Tweedie. She was a well-known feminist and a writer who lived in England. At that time, she used to write a weekly column on women's issues in the *Guardian*. She wrote, asking if I could help her, 'study a typical Indian woman'. I did not know her at all, and was somewhat irritated by the question. I knew that she wanted to meet a woman, who was one of the millions who are invisible. But she was obviously quite unaware of the complexity of India's social structure and cultural divides. I wrote to her giving her a variety of choices. Which class, which caste, from the north or south, east or west, urban or rural, literate or illiterate, working woman or a woman who is housebound, with or without political party affiliation, which language group . . . ? The list went on. Jill was perplexed and realized her mistake. She wrote back saying, 'A poor rural woman, preferably a Dalit; a working woman.' But the rest she left to me. When she came to spend some weeks in rural Rajasthan, we learnt enormous amounts from each other as we discussed feminist theory and politics, within an even larger global canvas of women's unique struggles against inequality.

Jill's question of an 'average Indian woman' inadvertently raised the Hydra-headed nature and the fractures within this broad category called 'women'. The subaltern, caste and religion, race, political ideological positions and regional prejudices, despite economic progress for larger numbers, continue to stay. The euphoria of gender collectivism often cracks under the pressure for privilege; the desire to conform and to maintain the status quo, and clutch to hierarchy. Nevertheless, the promise of the twin principles of equality and freedom in the Indian Constitution was inspiration enough, for organizing struggles for equality and justice in the democratic spaces of independent India.

So, Jill faced an overwhelming range of choices, trying to understand Indian women through a 'feminist lens'. It was a reflection of the extraordinary diversity, and huge numbers of ongoing struggles across India. Indian feminism cannot separate its vision from the multitude of the ongoing struggles against inequalities in caste, class, religion, region, the rural and urban, even when addressing gender inequalities. However, there are some that bond when there is violence on our bodies and the demand for peace and freedom. This bond defines our intermittent and underlying solidarity to shape a vision of Indian feminism.

Discrimination against women is universal. Even privileged women have had to understand oppression, and join collectives which have given them voice and space to fight for a wider vision of equality. They have strategically used their access to platforms of decision-making to challenge patriarchy and all its different structures of illegitimate power. Right from the initial days of the Indian republic, they have been able to get contentious issues tabled and even legislated. Most importantly, they have etched the right to question inequality and injustice as an undeniable part of the public discourse.

Money, class, privilege or proximity to patriarchal power structures did not succeed in fully diluting the early demands for equal rights. The dominant discourse was shaped therefore in multiple ways. Many transcended the barriers of class, caste and religion to help build the foundations of a women's movement in India. Even as a part of the independence movement, issues of social inequality and exploitative practices such as dowry, devadasi, sati, personal laws, women's right to property and land were taken up though they were not central to any debate. These formed the foundation for gender-based issues and continued to be part of the struggles in independent India. In some ways, the challenges were even greater, as most of the conventional political power went to men after Independence. As women faced marginalization from a very unrepresentative Parliament, they combined with many grass-roots groups and social movements to try and put in place a progressive legislative framework based on justice and equality. For a brief period of time, as laws did get passed, it looked as if a poor country would combine its urge to be upwardly mobile with progressive legislation that addressed all sections of the society, to rid itself of the stranglehold of restrictive traditions. But with the increasing commodification of women in the market economy, a new set of problems have cropped up that need to be addressed.

Social Movements in Independent India

The wider global and national political context has also had its impact. In these seventy years, India witnessed the principles and rhetoric of socialism yield to the profit-driven and so-called 'free market'. The assaults on the weak have continued through the change. Nevertheless, the capacity to recognize, to fight and to articulate individually and collectively is stronger today than it ever was. Marginalized groups such as women, Dalits and tribals began to come out, so to speak, and demand empowerment. The struggles of the marginalized have been intrinsic to and articulated better by social movements, than the often shallow rhetoric of political parties. Eventually, these movements have had some success in playing a progressive role in the face-off between the laws of a traditional hierarchical society and a developing legal framework under the Indian

Constitution. For an urban-born activist, working in rural India, the tangible and noticeable change has allowed me to internalize the value of collective principles so important to feminism and democracy.

There is no doubt that India has changed, and so have women's awareness and levels of self-confidence. Change is never uniform; as we face new challenges, we regress in some very significant areas. Modernism is more apparent in the symbols than in the real choices one can make. How else can we explain political choices for patriarchal leaders and their ideological systems even by large numbers of women today? This does not happen only with Trump. There are echoes in India as well.

Aspirations and Negotiations

As a young woman from a privileged segment of the Indian society, I grew up surrounded by the aspirations of a country awakening to democracy and freedom. The first phenomenon that seriously critiqued parliamentary democracy, for me, was the rising in Naxalbari. The age of innocence had come to an end.

In the civil service in the Lal Bahadur Shastri National Academy, I discovered the strength of women and the crude antipathy of the so-called crème de la crème as we battled gender prejudice. Some male fellow probationers simmered at the intrusion into what they felt was the male citadel of administrative power. This often pushed women officers to have to prove themselves in 'macho' terms. Feminist and humane values were dismissed as 'soft' and impractical. We watched one set of men replace the other year after year, the transition from feudalism and colonialism to patriarchal capitalism was subtly but smoothly perpetuated.

I came to live in rural Rajasthan after my initiation, or so I believed, to rural realities through the civil service. But it had simply not prepared me for an actual world revealed without the barriers of propriety.

Only the unabashed diktats of something like 'Manu Smriti' could help explain the unbelievable inequality visible in caste and gender. Some of the most extreme forms of exclusion, oppression and feudal exploitation were codified in outrageous forms of physical exclusion. The battle against untouchability and caste, the curse on a people, haunts India with its institutionalized violence and denial of basic humanity. It continues to live on, even as it is denied. It remains the first identity and the reason for every discrimination. The Dalit woman is at the bottom of that pile.

In reality, women covered their faces with thick cloth down to their navel, whispered in public, took off their shoes as they walked through the village; could not speak in the jati panchayat that discussed the fate of women. The hierarchy of heights and of postures was strictly followed—sitting on the village *chabutra* or on a chair to work the sewing machine was, and is even now, prohibited. Some women could not carry water for ablution and their biological needs. One man, a sarpanch in Ajmer district, during a meeting in Chota Naraina village, in 1975, publicly argued that a woman's life was worth less than a buffalo's, demanding a veterinary hospital instead of a health centre. It led to animated public argument between the women from outside and the men in the village. The women won the day, because of the silent consent of their gender. Most girls did not go to school. Many children died at birth, and a live child—especially a boy—was a celebration. There was bondage now in a more hidden form. Questions could only be raised by those who were in the preordained list—decided by the patriarchal and powerful in the feudal and caste hierarchy. Violence against women was treated casually, and domestic violence was almost taken for granted. There is change, but much more awaits our attention. Some of these practices of exclusion and discrimination still persist—coded within the metamorphosis to modernization. There is also a reactionary hardening of positions on caste and gender. Nevertheless, if I look back, there has probably been more change for women in the last forty years than in the 400 before.

The human desire for equality, justice and dignity is universal and indefatigable. Individually, no matter where they were in the hierarchy, the women I met were strong and straightforward. In fact, those who had faced oppression were stronger. I met women who questioned my universe in bits and pieces, including my approach to gender inequality and sexuality. Initially, they only saw difference, whereas—notwithstanding the disparities—I saw similarity. The conflicting views and the friendships from those struggling for change in urban as well as rural India began a process of unlearning, understanding and learning for me, and forced a new world on my new-found friends. A commentary about women in India will have to incorporate my conversations with the rural working-class feminist, as well as the urban feminist who has had the advantage of education and economic security. These different voices will have to be strung together.

My Conversations with Two Women

The feminist movement over the last seventy years has struggled to overcome the strong restrictions and limitations imposed on women and creatively explore the possibility of greater equality. In an effort to capture some of the richness of the nature of these journeys through seventy years of independent India, I bring to you my conversations with two very different women.

Even for me, it is important to understand change through the experiences of Naurti, a working-class Dalit woman. She is my peer in age and experience and an icon in Rajasthan. Ours is a narrative that tries to capture the potential of collective struggle, a living history of class, caste and gender struggles over the last four decades in rural India.

With Nandini—a young, concerned and thoughtful (twenty-five-year-old) feminist from a privileged urban home, my conversation takes me to the frontiers of the globalized world. She reflects on the many contradictions and conflicts faced by the younger, literate and 'educated' Indian woman. With her, I am able to explore some of the concerns of young modern feminists as they face the challenge of understanding and confronting the multiple inequalities of 'post neo-liberal' India. Somewhere between and around Naurti and Nandini is a fluid reality; which too, one would argue, is relative.

Women and Work—Naurti as a Labour Leader

To claim friendship with Naurti is a privilege. She helped initiate me into the struggles and lives of rural women who work in the fields and on worksites, and face without interpretation or gloss multiple forms of exclusion that people like me cannot even begin to imagine. Later, Naurti and I were to become comrades when she first struck with 500 fellow workers in her village, Harmara, in 1981. She went on to win a landmark Supreme Court case that held that no worker—man or woman—could be paid less than the statutory minimum wage. On the worksite where Naurti had organized the strike, men and women were paid substantially different wages for the same work. The understanding of women's struggles and their contribution to mainstream political thought came during my association with Naurti. The major preoccupation of millions of India's working women is access to work and food. The constant refrain of 'we want work' across Rajasthan and rural India led to the demand for the Mahatma Gandhi National Rural Employment Guarantee Act (MGNREGA), inspired by the Maharashtra Employment Guarantee Act that had been legislated in 1975.

Work is fundamental to well-being, a reverse of the dream of leisure that is often the preoccupation of women and men who are more affluent. The nature of the details of the formulation as well as many of the principles of the works programme came from rural working-class women and men. It explains why it raised the hackles of the rich urban elite. In spite of its best efforts, the current government has not been able to push the work programme off the priority of concerns. The women and men in India who sent the 10 million signatures to Delhi knew what they wanted and why. Women as providers and as those responsible for life and critical in staving off hunger were the prime movers of the MGNREGA.

Naurti campaigned for the MGNREGA, as an ardent advocate, on the street and in policy discussions. During an NDTV television debate in Delhi in 2005, she took on Surjit Bhalla, the economist, when he said a dole was much better—transfer cash to poor people's accounts—than have such a programme. Her answer to him was, 'I am willing to put my entire year's earnings in your bank account as your one month's salary, if you sit idle for a month so that you understand what a dole is. What we are demanding is the opposite of a dole.' Work is dignity, purpose and fulfilment.

Work as Liberation

While discussing feminism and the working class with Nandini, she made a specific reference to women like Naurti, for whom work was first a form of exploitation, with no practical opportunity for being able to move up the hierarchy. It was only much later, and with amazing organizational capacities, that Naurti managed to change her struggle into a series of rights and entitlements. Her question was:

Is there a disconnect between what I have studied on feminist theories of 'work' (linked to 'empowerment') and the lives of the women whose experiences have shaped your feminism? How does one reconcile the two?

The literate urban-based woman often goes through personal struggles, but the rural poor woman has to rely on collective strength for any form of empowerment. These experiences, whether personal or collective, play an even larger role in the formulations of feminist thought—no matter whether or not it is called 'feminism'. However, building feminist theory is not the domain of the literate woman alone; the more radical women's struggles for change have occurred amongst people who belong to the oral tradition. The woman who is a wage worker and peasant has addressed poverty and gender oppression. Her concerns and demand for equality pose a challenge for all struggles. They encapsulate the complex but universally relevant sets of multiple hierarchies that need to be questioned and changed. Formal feminist theories and writings did provide a framework to lodge questions that arose. But the theoretical framework was continually challenged as being inadequate and perhaps not inclusive enough. Women's work across the board is devalued by patriarchy. The demand for work is such a powerful idea that it resonates and potentially connects resistance to all forms of inequity and oppression.

Nandini's concern was also about understanding the specifics of discrimination across the barriers of class and education. The challenges faced by the urban woman who has to negotiate space in a spiralling, violent and inhospitable urban environment are formidable.

The issue of different perspectives dividing women that Nandini raised is certainly true even today. The answer is to build a wider and more meaningful alliance between different classes, castes, occupations and regional differences to reflect the plurality amongst us. The negotiation for workspace is likewise diverse. The urban working-class woman works as domestic, casual contract labour, battling multiple forms of inequality in the urban space: for security of employment, to protect herself from sexual assault, for space to live in a slum and fight the corrupt regulatory systems, beginning with the municipalities and the police. She is often a rural woman, who has come to the city searching for work, to eat and feed her family. Her politicization brought the two seemingly divergent issues together in the struggle for gender equality; it was both a political and economic battle.

Nandini's worry was that socialism and theories of class consciousness looked primarily at political liberation. The capitalist world saw the economic space outside home as contested space. Neither addressed many issues of society and its hierarchies which transcended class, and also slipped between the theoretical cracks.

The space outside home is still contested. The rural working-class woman worked outside her home. It was a natural and necessary part of her world, but that work was not recognized, either independently or as a primary contribution to the family vocation of pottery, leather work, agriculture, etc. On the other hand, politicization of the woman looking to break domestic bondage was a huge opportunity for the middle-class woman, fighting loneliness and social disapproval. The urban, educated woman had the challenge of dealing with personal competitiveness forcing lonely battles upon her, trapped despite talent, capability and self-expression.

In the last seventy years, Indian women have established their right to work in contested spaces outside the home. Recognition of their multiple forms of work and self-expression, from unpaid, uncounted work on farms and in family occupations to entering male citadels—being officers in the armed forces, or sarpanches, zila parishad members, ministers, chief ministers, prime ministers, pilots and drivers, professors and civil servants—is diverse and empowering. The discourse has likewise strengthened the issues of working women, often forcing public debate and even leading to new legislations. Women's organizations have been formed on the basis of employment concerns, political affiliations, gender oppression, professional interests and occupational hazards and requirements. These struggles in the last seven decades have firmly changed the way women are perceived.

We also need to pay attention to the new hazards, which come from a regressive, resurgent attempt to push women back into the constricting atmosphere of patriarchy and the family. There is a new form of political mobilization of women along religious and caste lines. This often runs parallel with invoking prejudices of religion and caste. *The World Before Her* is a disturbing film because it has chosen to depict two ends of the spectrum, and ignore the political relevance of the larger majority between the two. In a rural show, the women who had fought shackles at the cost of years of continued struggle took strong exception to being sandwiched between the less than 1 per cent of the women in contests for beauty queens and the slightly larger number using religion and violence as tools. They stated that it also devalued their belief that India is now a victim to polarized debates that leave little room for genuine negotiation and peace.

Political Representation and Reservation

Bhim Rao Ambedkar and Savitribai Phule needed access to real education to be able to question the sanctity of caste and gender hierarchies. Ambedkar's call to 'educate, organize, agitate' encapsulates the struggle for equality in a hierarchical culture. For them work was survival and political power was the only passport to dignity. The struggles in the Dalit movement brought a realization that real empowerment comes through both platforms of democratic expression—organized collective struggle and articulation—and representation through the vote. Where is women's representation in this lexicon of political representation and empowerment?

Figures of women's representation in our legislatures are shameful: A UN report in the year 2017 states that India is 148th of 193 countries in the matter of women's representation. In the Lok Sabha with only sixty-two women out 542 members, India 'boasts' 11.8 per cent women's representation, far below the 23 per cent average of the world. Rwanda has 61.3 per cent, Bolivia 53 per cent and Cuba 48.9 per cent women in Parliament. In the Indian Rajya Sabha also women's representation is 11 per cent. Yet, these figures have not led to a national concern to immediately take corrective measures.

Rural Women and the Vote—Naurti as a Political Leader

The real shift in the possibilities of equality in public office in India came with the limited but important Seventy-third and Seventy-fourth Amendments (1993) to the Constitution of India. This made provisions for reservation of seats in the local bodies of panchayats and municipalities for tribals, Dalits, OBCs and women, laying a strong foundation for their participation in decision-making at the local levels. In Rajasthan, for instance, there is 50 per cent reservation for women, with a rotation amongst women for OBC and Dalit candidates. It was quite revolutionary to see a Dalit woman sit on the chair of the sarpanch. In one stroke, she actually and metaphorically claimed equality. Even just as a symbol, it was a very powerful one. It is obvious that without reservation, marginalized communities have little or no hope of representation. Reservation has been a touchy issue for the privileged, chary of sharing their abundance—be it reservation for Dalits or women. An attempt to address inequality is seen as appeasement, as in the case of minority communities. The upper-caste critique of reservation alleges devaluation of excellence and capability, based on patriarchal values.

Women's participation in public space was first as workers contributing to the economy and later as voters. But it would have been impossible to overcome more than millennia of entrenched patriarchy without reservation in education, work and representation. Naurti entered the fray and fought two elections. With reservation introduced in panchayats, she won with a huge majority in 2010 to become sarpanch and ran a much better and more transparent panchayat. Expenditure was painted on the walls for all to see. Encroachments by the powerful were cleared. Large numbers of development works were undertaken. Some corrupt people were caught and were sent to jail. She taught the secretary and the computer operator of her panchayat how to access the NREGA website. She paid special attention to the needs of women and looked at issues of dignity, not just for Dalits but also for minorities.

Naurti was one of the many important leaders of the Right to Information campaign. Her initial efforts to access information from her sarpanch in 1997 resulted in a false case of assault. She is still battling it in court.

And yet elite capture lurked round the corner. She was debarred from standing for election through an ordinance and then a law. She is now a petitioner in a Supreme Court case, challenging the law introduced and passed by the Vasundhara Raje government that all those who have not passed 8th standard cannot stand for election as sarpanch!

Women with forty years of experience in dealing with panchayat-level governance issues are better suited to prevent mismanagement of public funds than the younger group, because of their understanding of public issues. Such women are now handicapped by not having school certificates. Schools were not accessible to women of Naurti's generation. The failure of delivery of educational services has made Naurti a victim twice: First for being denied access to education and then denying her eligibility for contesting elections! Struggling for justice and placing contentious issues in the public domain are not taught in schools, where the status quo is strictly protected. The state governments as well as the Centre proudly tout formal learning as an unnecessary criterion for choosing ministers, appointing school-leavers to manage higher education and oversee policy. Why then should the panchayat, which works largely with the oral tradition, where matters are understood by everyone, be outside the reach of mature women without Class VIII school certificates?

While reservation in panchayats came with the Seventy-third Amendment, Parliament operates with claim to a different logic. There is no educational qualification and no reservation for women. What needed to be questioned and sought was a move away from mere representation, to real participation. This shift is best articulated by the feminist movement, which had powerful Indian reinterpretations.

The figures revealed by the UN should have galvanized us to act. A women's reservation bill has been pending in Parliament for the last twenty years. However, even today, there is little hope of its passage.

Feminism in Modern Times: A Lens of Equality and Common Sense

In this age of trade, profit and loss, where value is equated to material benefits alone, the issue of women and their equality has acquired all the qualities of the times. It is a much more difficult battle for those of us fighting the feudal patriarchal past, now happily married to its modern cousin—consumerism. In modern capitalist times too women alone are sold, with sexist evaluations of capital, investment and profitability. Our status is proportionate to our market value. We are now protesting against being bought, sold and used as an asset or a commodity, in the social, political and economic spheres.

This leads to new challenges facing Indian feminism—particularly for those of us who are conscious of inequality not in economic terms alone. Who ties our price tags and then promotes our sales? And why are we so easily seduced to surrender to 'fair and lovely', and the many ways in which our bodies are shaped, misshaped and constricted, changed to please the buyer? In these chaotic times, what else thwarts different efforts to set right the simple demand to be equal? The attack on women's bodies is proportionate to her visibility and empowerment. The market has made her a commodity to be used and discarded. To increase her price commensurate with her status, the market has produced a variety of lures so that she becomes the victim of her own ambitions, flattered by ads and humiliated to please the ego of patriarchy.

Feminism gave birth to the powerful slogan of 'the personal is political'. Nandini pointed out in her conversation that the need to theorize about family, motherhood and sexuality has been felt by women in the private and the public spheres. The acknowledgement that the 'personal is political' is inherent in women's personal lives and struggles. The slogan provided a unique and powerful framework that linked the two, making it one of the most important and evocative contributions of and to feminist thought. Naurti also acknowledged its importance; it translated into looking at the politics in each one of her expressions. Each action could now be examined for itself, without being seen through a shifting lens of traditional acceptance of inequality—caste, gender, class and so on. Today, after we thought the struggle was over, we begin to struggle all over again, amongst other things, against the image of woman as 'devi', housebound and 'protected': an elevation which confines her to stay unquestioning on the pedestal of patriarchy!

As one begins to understand the nature of Right-wing conservative politics, the relationship between the personal and the political is even more crucial, but needs to be understood in its broadest sense. After years of struggle in India, women have been able to wrench the right of choice of a partner in marriage in some select cases. The targeting of women through calculated attacks like love jihad and khap panchayats disempower women, keeping them away from fundamental freedom and secular rights as citizens in a democracy. As victims of the politics of a rising fundamentalism, it satisfies the users of religion to get political mileage and power, and ensure that women are repeatedly fragmented and controlled as bits of property in a male-dominated society. The personal also has to be 'social', where social codes of the past and the norms of the modern 'market' have to be confronted.

It is only this comprehensive relationship of gender that will give the feminist movement an opportunity to provide solidarity to all women fighting oppression and inequality in India. Social movements in India have in some ways attempted to forge this kind of understanding.

Where the Social, the Political and the Market Meet: Social Movements and Change

Women's fight for equality often begins with very personal issues. In women's struggles, the 'I' has changed quickly to 'our'. It has also made the ruthless examination of personal choices an inevitable part of the political discourse. Revolutionary change becomes more reachable, personal and immediately political when we say 'my life is a revolution'. The feminist understanding of radical change that emerges denies us the luxury of procrastination, to wait for the revolution. As women, we have a much greater personal responsibility for creative resistance and change. It encompasses the continual dialectic of the personal embedded in political structures. In addition, it provides a framework for the individual to be connected to larger movements for change. Most importantly, it draws on the relationship of one's own courage to change the society. As women in a Dhaka workshop composed and sang: '*Tu khud ko badal, tu khud ko badal, tabhi to jamana badlega.*'

The Emotional Is Expression of Personal Angst, and the Angst Is Political

This popular opinion that women are 'emotional, passionate' and therefore incapable, vulnerable and illogical is a patriarchal myth. Nandini raised the issue in her conversations and despite the many years that separate us, the language of suppression finds continuity. In our creative resistance, how do we avoid becoming defensive and end up subscribing to a narrow 'macho' definition of rationality. Rationality is not the opposite of 'emotional'. When there is a conflict between the emotional and unemotional in the patriarchal public domain, the male expression as unemotional is projected as being logical even if it is based on years of prejudiced, mindless repression. The demand for freedom to choose is confused with stereotypes projected to denigrate the 'liberated' woman—apparel or hairstyle, *'bal katti aurtein'*. Patriarchy damns the manner of expression to escape culpability for perpetuating inequality. Feminism does not believe that 'manliness' is a virtue.

The feminist perception of the universe in securing peace is so much more 'rational' than the world dominated by so-called 'rational' men who want destruction and war! It is a world view where equality is the basis to bring harmony, rather than conflict. The assumption was that the feminine must define itself and celebrate its being. We even defined the protagonist as 'the intimate enemy'. In other words we have to resolve a dichotomy, ever present, and therefore create a new lexicon.

The subtle combination of patriarchy and the market has pushed the liberating ideas and processes down the hole of revival of fears—through superstitions such as witches (*dakan*s), religious malpractices and the greed for an affluent, acquisitive society. The films, advertisements, the redefinition of fashion and design have given space for the revival of gender inequality and patriarchy.

Women can, and do, assimilate patriarchal values. At first as a need to survive, and later to enjoy their share of the fruits of position gained and authority exercised. They too have been 'persuaded' to internalize those values. It is a challenge that has been met and continues to be addressed. But we must not forget that the nature of a constant vigilante macho society makes women in leadership roles more vulnerable than their male counterparts.

The Role of Progressive Laws and the Constitutional Framework

Like all other movements of the marginalized, women have had to continually interpret social, political and economic norms through the lens of equality and justice in the Indian Constitution. In India class and caste divides that would estrange women from time to time, came together in the many significant struggles we have fought and won, principally on our bodies. Laws were passed for the abolition of sati, dowry, the labelling and persecution of witches and female feticide to name a few. The law to prevent, investigate and prosecute rape, molestation and sexual harassment in the workplace or at home has been substantially strengthened through a participatory process. Violence against women is an issue on which the bulk of Indian women have come together, except for the stark self-exclusion of the ultra-traditional Right and, to some extent, the extremist Left.

And yet for some, the rule of law, including these laws, is a distant dream. The brutality of rape and violence is more visible now than ever before. From Bhanwari's case of gang rape, when the national conscience was made to respond, to the horror of the Nirbhaya rape, bestiality, irreverence for any moral or legal code continues to hang as a threat. The rape law is conciliation by the state. But the corruption of regulatory mechanisms and the lack of any action on such issues bring back the divisive nature of Indian society and the corruption and arbitrary use of power in governance.

As the young look at the third-generation problems of violence on their bodies, the revival of pernicious customs like sati, *dakinis/dayans* (witches), regressive platforms for decision-making such as khap panchayats and jati panchayats, and reactionary social movements like 'ghar vapsi' and 'love jihad' attempt to take away all choice and impose majoritarian social norms through brute force and violence. This makes the day-to-day struggles of those wanting to break free of these traditional laws much more dangerous and difficult. Large numbers of women, still caught in traditional caste-based geography of patriarchal rule, would find it difficult to imagine the great strides Indian women—mothers and grandmothers—have made to inch closer to the promise of constitutional equality.

There have been old and new formations and alliances made to face these threats. NFIW, AIDWA, All India Mahila Congress, AIPWA are progressive national mass-based women's organizations built broadly on party lines and with ideological commitments. 'The Pinjra Tod' campaign, the campaign to 'Reclaim the Streets', or the international 'One Billion Rising' (OBR) are some of the many large mobilizations of women seeking to exercise equality and choice. The powerful local and rural women's groups mushrooming since the early 1970s are often initiators of important issues of working-class women, such as wages, rape, sati, against reviving the mirage of witchery.

Women are in the forefront of the right to food and right to work campaigns, as they are in movements against genetic modification of seeds, UID, 377 IPC, anti-nuclear campaign, and movements for Dalit rights, minority rights, protection of forest and tribal rights. They have to take on the might of groups and political leaders who want to use religious and social laws to perpetuate their power and privilege in every sphere.

Their access to important positions of executive office has raised fundamental questions about their ability to deal with the contradiction between upholding constitutional values and the dictates of office—corrupt and using arbitrary power to claim impunity from all accountability. Battles will now have to be fought for protecting the Constitution and seeking accountability to implement hard-won laws.

The macho leadership—in the US and India amongst others—getting more jingoistic by the minute, is raising the ghosts of hate and division amongst people to get popular mandates. At this time the world begs for values of equality, justice, peace, compassion and tolerance. The principles of democracy have been hollowed out to keep the skeleton of electoral systems, using it to aggrandize power without accountability. Women's participation in public life, we hope, will be able to bring back the values we have lost in relationships, family, society, between nations, with people who are different and the body politic.

Naurti, Nandini and I met as women from different spheres of Indian womanhood to agree that these values are certainly worth struggling for. Women will continue to reach out, as we have always done, to form greater collectives to assert our right to equality, free expression, transparency, accountability and the right to live with dignity and justice. As we strengthen each other, we resolve that to surrender is suicide.

—With Naurti Devi and Nandini Dey, and all the women I have learnt from . . .

Negotiations

SHABANA AZMI

Shabana Azmi, a renowned actor who has worked in over 140 Indian and several international films, is a former member of Parliament and a social activist working for the rights of women, children and slum dwellers. She is a strong voice against religious fundamentalism. Azmi believes that art should be used as an instrument for social change.

The idea of India is such a lofty title—seems impossible to encapsulate in a few pages—but its strength lies in the fact that it means different things to different people. India is more than the sum of its parts, and its raison d'être lies in its contradictions.

India is a country that lives in several centuries simultaneously. Her people, at any given time and place, encapsulate all the contradictions that come from being a multicultural, multi-religious and multilingual country. Whatever claim you make in India, its opposite is equally true, as Shashi Tharoor famously says.

India, which constitutes about one-seventh of the world's population, probably also contributes towards one-seventh of its discrimination. While the magnitude of India's problems—including discrimination—is of mammoth size, equally large and exciting is her potential. The holistic picture of India is difficult to fathom, generating an inward-looking spate of literature recently, about imagining and reimagining India.

The nation of India is new but the notion of India is rather ancient. It is an amalgam of its essence, image and value: the essence is of oneness, the image is of contradictions and the value is *kartavya* or duty. The contradiction resides in each one of us. We Indians yearn for unity, respect and sacrifice but often seem to spread chaos.

I work in the glamorous film world of Mumbai, which very often lives by the motto that excess is success. I also belong to my father's village, Mijwan (in eastern Uttar Pradesh), which lives in the fear of an uncertain tomorrow. As I work in both these places, I travel in time, traversing centuries into the past between Mumbai and Mijwan in less than twenty-four hours. Such contrast envelops India in manifold dimensions.

India is the silence of meditation embedded in the muted serenity of the Himalayas. It is also a cacophony: loud weddings, louder prayers, honking horns and shouting TV anchors.

India exudes beauty: the white symmetry of the Taj Mahal, vibrancy of Madhubani, colours of Kutch, carvings of Konark. Yet India is an eyesore: garbage mounds, discarded plastic bags and railway-line defecators.

India is an olfactory assault: smoky air, putrid drains and burning cow dung. But there is also the fragrance of Alfonso, the smell of coconut and the seduction of '*ittar*'.

India is a story of lost opportunities and an unresponsive system of governance; the abode of the illiterate, the poor, the blind and the sick. But India is also dreams and soaring aspirations of the young, the energy of entrepreneurs and the feisty spirit of voluntary organizations.

India teems with callous urbanites, bribe-seeking 'babus'. At the same time, it offers hope with democracy, a constitution and an independent judiciary.

India assaults one's sensibility with its urban malls faking progress and the rural markets begging progress; with its woman abusers walking with impunity among the goddess worshippers; with starving children living next to warehouses bulging with rotting food.

How does one negotiate such disruptive contradictions with India's ability to thrive? How has India traversed millennia as the longest surviving civilization in the world?

Perhaps, it is largely due to the fact that some of the wisest thoughts for humanity have emanated from the astute minds of this land, which have rescued us from demise.

Probably, one of India's most profound contributions to the world of thought is the concept of non-duality of existence. Simply put, it enunciates the fact that we all are connected, inseparable and indistinguishable at a fundamental level: you, I and the whole universe. However, it is an impediment in our perception—an illusion—which makes us feel separate, split and unequal. The natural corollary of oneness is equality, not only among men but also with nature. This imperceptible, invisible DNA has guided the existence of India.

This thought of oneness has endured centuries and has become the core value of our nation, a part of our being. It has manifested in our history in many ways. Our syncretic culture, openness to alien ideas and people, and worshipful respect for nature have been some of the defining features.

We have, unfortunately, relegated this profound thought to the spiritual world and failed to propagate it as a political thought. The responsibility to create a society based on the principle of oneness has been left to seers and sages. Buddha,

Nanak, Chishti, Kabir, Vivekananda, Bulleh Shah and many others tried to steer us to the basics. While we have succeeded in creating prayer halls to perpetuate their names, we have failed to follow their ideals.

Our historical drawback has been the inability to create a polity based on the idea of oneness. Ashoka, Akbar and probably other lesser-known kings gave it a try but could not sustain it. Monarchy is contradictory to equality and oneness. Equality needs democracy.

It is then not an accident that the wise fathers of modern India kept this oneness as the running theme of our Constitution and gave us a democratic republic. India became a promise— still a work in progress—of a democratic nation, bestowing equality, justice and freedom. Indians accepted this promise as immutable, sacred and supreme. It granted us rights and also demanded responsibility.

To demand our rights, our intellect has developed modern narratives to comprehend the complex world by breaking it into smaller pieces such as religions, creeds, classes and genders. We have learnt to analyse the complex world with tools of capitalism, communism, socialism, feminism and fundamental rights. These paradigms have encouraged us to consider human history as a continual conflict between competing power groups. This process empowers one section of the society at the cost of the others.

Because of inherently competing stances, these tools encourage dissension, which becomes a source of genuine power for leaders in a democracy. The modern analytical tools to understand people, however, have often led to conflict creation and not its resolution. Conflict merely for the sake of power is a dangerous weapon in the hands of usurpers, many of whom thrive in the Indian democracy. The poison of creed and greed is defining their current discourse.

But the Constitution demands responsibility as much as it grants rights. Our responsibility as citizens is to improve our ability to see the whole and not just the parts. We need new tools that synthesize social responsibility and don't merely analyse individual rights. Modern times have thrown a challenge to the wise of our land, to devise new devices and institutions that unite and don't divide.

One kind of institution that has taken deep roots is the not-for-profit non-government organization or the NGO. India has the largest number of NGOs in the world. A government survey in 2008 counted 3.3 million or 33 lakh registered NGOs in the country, and probably many more have sprung up since then. This is not counting the unregistered voluntary organizations. This staggering number amounts to one NGO for every 400 Indians. Even if 99 per cent of these NGOs are malfunctioning or dysfunctional, we are still left with one NGO for every 40,000 citizens.

We have crossed the critical mass. We have enough volunteers in the society to transform India in less than ten years. The imperceptible growth of this transformational force was driven by the same essence of India which inspired our Constitution: that of responsibility, duty and sacrifice. It is not new. It started much before you and me, for the essence of India was alive then as it is now.

The idea of India that has kept us going for a few 1000 years was alive a 100 years ago and is thriving through responsible citizens today. But it is not enough to count our virtues and vices. We must explore the means of achieving our promise. And this is not an alien thought but has germinated in this land: The idea of *karsavina* or duty or responsibility. Our epics talk of responsibility. Our ancient values spoke of responsibility: towards our family, society and nature. We have been more a culture of responsibility and less of rights. Somewhere along the way, we supplanted the ideal of responsibility with a demand for expedient rights. We outsourced solutions to an external agency and gave up charge to improve our lot. It is time to reclaim our place under the sun.

Civil society has a very important role to play, both in providing support and putting up stiff resistance to any effort that is directed towards silencing voices.

To me the idea of India is simple. She is a secular, democratic republic, and her greatest strength is her composite culture— her 'Ganga-Jamuni tehzeeb'.

I was raised in a commune-like flat of a communist party, not surprisingly called The Red Flag Hall. Comrades like the great Urdu poet Ali Sardar Jafri, my father Kaifi Azmi and eight other families had just one small 280 sq. ft room each with a strip of a balcony that was converted into the kitchen. Eight families lived together with just one bathroom and one toilet. My father was a party whole-timer, and he would get a meagre Rs 40 to look after my mother, my brother and me. So there was never any money but it didn't seem to matter at all because the residents of Red Flag Hall were tuned to the sound of a different drummer, they were committed to a larger goal. They were determined to struggle for social justice, gender sensitivity and celebration of India's composite culture. All festivals were celebrated with much fanfare—Holi, Diwali, Eid, Christmas. As kids we were taken to the Sarvajanik Ganesh pandals and sang Christmas carols in school. On 26 January we would be put in a truck and taken to see the lights at Chowpatty; we imbibed India's pluralism almost through a process of osmosis.

Today, however, that pluralism seems to be under tremendous threat. Communalism is raising its ugly head and permeating into all strata of the society. Religion is being used by fundamentalists of all hues to divide people for narrow political gain. History is being rewritten to enumerate grievances of the past, both real and imaginary, that are sought to be corrected in the present and become the means of contemporary political mobilization. Any criticism of the state is labelled as anti-national, and the anonymity of social media is being used to systematically subdue robust resistance into silence by pushing dissenting voices into the binary of 'either you are with us or against us'. Mobocracy is threatening the very tenets of democracy and much more needs to be done to stem the rot. We need to recognize the signs of danger around us. It is said that if you put a frog in a cauldron of boiling water, it jumps out and saves itself. But if you put it in tepid water and gradually turn the temperature on, the frog doesn't realize it till it is too late and dies. We are like frogs who don't realize that the temperature around us is on a rise and very soon it might be too late.

If you ask me who I am, I will say that I am a woman, an Indian, a daughter, a wife, an actor, a Muslim and a Mumbaikar at the same time. My being Muslim is only one aspect of my identity, and yet today it seems as though a concerted effort is being made to compress identity into the narrow confines of the religion one was born into at the cost of all other identities!

So suddenly I have the word 'Muslim' hurled at me either as an accusation or with kid gloves—it makes me self-conscious in a way I have never experienced before. To argue that there is a pan-Islamic identity that subsumes all identities is factually incorrect. Islam resides in more than fifty-three countries in the world and takes on the culture of the country in which it is practised. So it is liberal in some countries, it is moderate in a few states and it is intolerant in some others. To paint all Muslims as one would be negating the complex layers of culture in shaping a person's identity. I am not a practising Muslim. There was an absence of religious indoctrination in the house. For me being a Muslim means biryani, Eid, the Urdu language and my Ganga-Jamuni tehzeeb, my composite culture.

I am an Indian Muslim, and I feel no affinity to the Saudi Arabian Muslims. I feel much closer to my Indian–Hindu, Indian–Christian and Indian–Sikh friends. What I have in common with them is a shared history, a shared identity and a shared future. As a Muslim in India, because I live in a democracy, I have a stake and a claim in aspiring to be the president of India, a world famous cricketer, a global film star, a successful entrepreneur because I have the space and the opportunity to dream and the wherewithal to attain it. Nevertheless, everything is not that hunky-dory. There are problems like there are anywhere in the world. However, there is a robust resistance to discrimination by an active civil society that gives me the strength to speak my mind. Do not box me in, do not try to restrict me in the desire 'to integrate'. For narrow political gain, do not polarize the atmosphere and force people to create a 'model community'—a model community of either women, Dalits, tribals or any other label that can be used to make me feel like 'the other'. What stands true for me stands true everywhere in the world, whether in Britain or in the US or in any country that calls itself a democracy.

We must all work to remove the construct of 'the other': the other gender, the other race, the other nation, the other religion. But this is a construct; it is not the truth of India—India's greatest identity is her composite culture. A Kashmiri Hindu and a Kashmiri Muslim have much more in common with each other because of their cultural identity, their Kashmiriyat, than a Kashmiri Muslim and a Muslim from Tamil Nadu in spite of the fact that they share a common religion.

We are fearful of the unknown. And that's where culture becomes the most effective means of understanding a people. Not so long ago, it was not uncommon for Indians to be asked whether they still lived in trees or whether bullock carts in cities were still the only mode of transport. And we are equally guilty of being ignorant of other cultures. But the world is changing and the time is ripe for us to seize the opportunity with both hands. The advent of technology, satellite television, the explosion of the social media are lifting the shrouds in which cultures were denied visibility.

As an artiste I seek to use my art to soothe, to excite, to provoke, to entertain because I believe art has the ability to create a climate of sensitivity in which it is possible for change to occur.

There is much that needs our attention if we want the idea of India to flourish. As India seeks to become a global power, we must also pause to ask which model of development needs to be pursued. Whose development and at whose cost is a question that begs to be answered. It cannot be the progress of a few at the cost of many. One of India's greatest challenges to me is that large infrastructure projects need to be put in place to drive the engines of growth, but this will lead to displacement of large numbers of people. Unless the principle of social justice is applied to resettling the displaced, no genuine development will be possible; in fact there will be social unrest and chaos as has been witnessed in Nandigram and other places. A project-affected person might ask, 'If I am displaced from the land of my birth for "the greater common good", then surely I have the right to be the first beneficiary of that project or at least one of the beneficiaries?' Alas, such is not the case as experience shows. We need economic progress without doubt but the benefits also need to reach those sections of India where 'the sun is not shining'.

Women are breaking their silence, women are speaking the language of rights. Women are freeing themselves from the stranglehold of a patriarchal society and demanding equality of opportunity to rise to the full level of their potential. With the Seventy-fourth Amendment a silent revolution is taking place and women are participating in the decision-making process. In Mijwan, a tiny village in UP's Azamgarh, where I work, girls as young as eight and women as old as eighty are saying girls are equal to boys. Girls are refusing to be pushed into marriage before the age of eighteen and are aspiring to work and become self-sufficient.

The major idea of India is inclusion; men and women, poor and rich, old and young, rural and urban—all must become active participants in the polity that strives for equity, justice, agency and empowerment.

India is not a melting pot in which individual identities are submerged. Instead India is a colourful mosaic in which individual identities are retained while contributing to a larger whole.

India is in the air I breathe. India is in the fragrance of the *mogra*, India is in the poetry of Kabir, Ghalib and Tagore.

India will always remain more than the sum of its parts.

Acknowledgements

This book is my first tentative foray into writing and hopefully more will follow. I have many people to thank for pushing me to do this, despite the crazy 24x7 life of a television journalist. Thank you to Meru Gokhale and Premanka Goswami of Penguin for coming up with the idea for the book and holding my hand through it all. Premanka has been an amazing editor. Thank you to all the contributors who not only wrote thoughtful pieces but were kind to me as I hassled them to meet the deadline! Each piece stands out and is written from the heart. Thank you to my parents for always being so supportive. A big thank you to Prannoy and Radhika Roy for all their support and for upholding the finest values of journalism. There are those who shall remain nameless for their support and encouragement (you know who you are). And finally, thank you, Hobbes.